Crypto Simplified:

A Beginner's Guide to Understanding Bitcoin, Blockchain, and Cryptocurrency Investing

Get Started On Your Journey To The Future Of Money

KENNETH K. LEE

Crypto Simplified: A Beginner's Guide to Understanding Bitcoin, Blockchain, and Cryptocurrency Investing - by Kenneth K. Lee

Published by Truniverse Media

Copyright © 2024 by Kenneth K. Lee

All rights reserved. You may neither reproduce nor transmit any part of the contents of this book in any form or by any means, without the written permission of the publisher.

Although the publisher and the author have tried to ensure that the information in this book was correct at press time and while this publication provides accurate information regarding the subject covered, the publisher and the author assume no responsibility for errors, inaccuracies, omissions, or any other inconsistencies and disclaim any liability to any party for any loss, damage, or disruption caused by errors or omissions, whether such errors or omissions result from negligence, accident, or any other cause.

Printed and bound in the United States of America

First Printing

Crypto Simplified: A Beginner's Guide to Understanding Bitcoin, Blockchain, and Cryptocurrency Investing - by Kenneth K. Lee

Disclaimers:

NOT FINANCIAL ADVICE

The information provided in this book is for educational and informational purposes only. It is not intended to be a substitute for professional financial advice, consultation, or endorsement of any kind. The author and the publisher are not financial advisors and make no representations or warranties, expressed or implied, as to the accuracy, completeness, or suitability of the information provided in this book.

Cryptocurrency investments are volatile and risky by nature. You should consult with a qualified financial advisor or conduct your own independent research and analysis before making any financial decisions or investments based on the contents of this book. Neither the author nor the publisher shall be liable for any loss, damage, or adverse consequences alleged to have occurred directly or indirectly as a result of the material in this book.

USE OF AI TECHNOLOGY

This book was created with the assistance of artificial intelligence to facilitate the research and drafting processes. However, it is important to note that the content has been extensively reviewed, edited, and personalized by the author. Any opinions, insights, or recommendations are solely those of the author and do not reflect the views of the AI or its developers.

The use of AI technology was intended to enhance the creative process and provide supplementary information where needed. While every effort has been made to ensure the accuracy and completeness of the content, the ultimate responsibility for the final published material rests with the author.

Crypto Simplified: A Beginner's Guide to Understanding Bitcoin, Blockchain, and Cryptocurrency Investing - by Kenneth K. Lee

Thank you for your understanding, and happy reading!

Crypto Simplified: A Beginner's Guide to Understanding Bitcoin, Blockchain, and Cryptocurrency Investing - by Kenneth K. Lee

Table of Contents

Introduction 10
    Who This Book Is For 11
    What You Will Learn 12
Part I: The Birth of Money and Currency 14
    Section 1: Introduction to Money and Currency 15
        1.1 The Basics of Money 16
        1.2 The Evolution of Money 17
        1.3 Modern-Day Money 18
        1.4 What is Currency? 19
        1.5 Types of Currency 20
        1.6 Transition from Physical to Digital Currency 22
        1.7 Key Takeaways 26
    Section 2: Traditional Financial Systems 27
        2.1 Banks and Financial Institutions 27
        2.2 The Stock Market 29
        2.3 Government and Money 30
        2.4 Problems with Traditional Systems 31
        2.5 Key Takeaways 33
Part II: The World of Bitcoin and Cryptocurrencies 34
    Section 3: What is a Cryptocurrency? 35
        3.1 Definition and Origin 35
        3.2 How It Differs from Traditional Currency 37
        3.3 Key Takeaways 38
    Section 4: Introduction to Bitcoin 39
        4.1 What is Bitcoin and how does it work? 39

4.2 Brief History and Its Creator 41
4.3 Bitcoin Mining 42
4.4 Use-Cases for Bitcoin 43
4.5 Bitcoin Storage Options 44
4.6 Key Takeaways 46

Section 5: Beyond Bitcoin - Altcoins, Tokens, NFTs 47
5.1 What Are Altcoins? 48
5.2 Notable Altcoins 51
5.3 ICOs and Tokens 61
5.4 The Rise of NFTs 63
5.5 Key Takeaways 65

Part III: Understanding Blockchain Technology 66
Section 6: Blockchain: The Technology Behind Cryptocurrency
.... 67
6.1 The Basics of a Blockchain 69
6.2 How Blocks and Chains Work 71
6.3 Importance of Blockchain in Cryptocurrency 74
6.4 Decentralization 77
6.5 Public vs Private Blockchains 79
6.6 Key Takeaways 83

Section 7: Blockchain Use-Cases 85
7.1 Financial Services 87
7.2 Supply Chain Management 89
7.3 Healthcare 91
7.4 Voting and Governance 94
7.5 Real Estate 96
7.6 Beyond Currency 98

7.7 Key Takeaways 100

Part IV: Getting Started With Cryptocurrencies 103

   Section 8: How to Buy Cryptocurrency.................................104

      8.1 Exchanges 106

      8.2 P2P Transactions 109

      8.3 ATMs 111

      8.4 Key Takeaways 113

   Section 9: Setting Up a Crypto Wallet 115

      9.1 Types of Wallets 117

      9.2 How to Set Up a Wallet...120

      9.3 Security Measures 123

      9.4 Key Takeaways 126

   Section 10: Understanding Public and Private Keys...........128

      10.1 What They Are..129

      10.2 Why They Are Important...132

      10.3 Key Takeaways 134

   Section 11: Cryptocurrency Mining 136

      11.1 What is Cryptocurrency Mining?..............................137

      11.2 How Does It Work?..141

      11.3 Is It Profitable for Beginners? 144

      11.4 Key Takeaways 147

Part V: Investing & Trading 149

   Section 12: Why Invest in Cryptocurrencies?......................150

      12.1 Potential for High Returns.......................................151

      12.2 Diversification 154

      12.3 Financial Sovereignty 158

      12.4 Key Takeaways 161

- Section 13: Basic Investment Strategies 164
  - 13.1 HODLing 165
  - 13.2 Active Trading 168
  - 13.3 Dollar-Cost Averaging 170
  - 13.4 Key Takeaways 173
- Section 14: How to Analyze a Cryptocurrency 175
  - 14.1 Market Cap 176
  - 14.2 Volume 179
  - 14.3 Price Charts 181
  - 14.4 Key Takeaways 184
- Section 15: Understanding Risks and Volatility 186
  - 15.1 Market Volatility 187
  - 15.2 Regulatory Risks 190
  - 15.3 Security Risks 192
  - 15.4 How to Be a Responsible Investor 195
  - 15.5 Key Takeaways 199
- Section 16: Taxes and Regulations 201
  - 16.1 Tax obligations 203
  - 16.2 Regulatory landscape 205
  - 16.3 Key Takeaways 208

Part VI: Beyond Basics 211
- Section 17: Smart Contracts and Decentralized Applications (DApps) 212
  - 17.1 What Are They? 213
  - 17.2 Real-World Examples 216
  - 17.3 Key Takeaways 219
- Section 18: Initial Coin Offerings (ICOs) and Tokens 222

- 18.1 What is an ICO? 224
- 18.2 How to Participate 227
- 18.3 Key Takeaways 230
- Section 19: The Future of Cryptocurrencies and Blockchain 233
  - 19.1 Upcoming Developments 235
  - 19.2 Government and Regulation 238
  - 19.3 Adoption and Acceptance 241
  - 19.4 Challenges Ahead 244
  - 19.5 Key Takeaways 247
- Section 20: Your Next Steps 250
  - 20.1 Learning Resources 252
  - 20.2 How to Buy Your First Crypto 255
  - 20.3 Where to Find Reliable Information 258
  - 20.4 How to Keep Learning 262
  - 20.5 Key Takeaways 265
- Conclusion 268
  - Final Thoughts 270
  - Next Steps 272
- Glossary 275
- Appendices 281
- Final Words 287

Crypto Simplified: A Beginner's Guide to Understanding Bitcoin, Blockchain, and Cryptocurrency Investing - by Kenneth K. Lee

Introduction

Welcome to the world of Crypto! You picked this book because you want to learn more about how the world of finance is around us and how digital money has changed. By doing so, you have now stepped foot in the fascinating world of cryptocurrencies. You've probably heard words like "Bitcoin," "blockchain," and "crypto" thrown around and wondered, "What's all the fuss about?" Well, you're in the right place to find out. This book aims to unravel the mysteries of cryptocurrency in a way that's engaging, accessible, and—most importantly—easy to understand.

Let's start by acknowledging that we're standing at the edge of financial history. We are witnessing a monetary revolution that could very well be as monumental as the invention of paper money. Cryptocurrency isn't just a new way to pay for things; it's a disruption, a challenge to the way we think about and use money. From how we buy our morning coffee to how nations conduct international trade, cryptocurrency is reshaping the rules.

However, it is important to consider why you should care before we get started. Maybe you're not a techie or a financial guru. Maybe terms like "distributed ledger" and "hash rate" make your eyes glaze over. That's okay! You don't need to be an expert to understand why cryptocurrency matters. Think about the first time you sent an email or made an online purchase. You didn't need to know the technicalities of how it worked; you just needed to know that it did. The same goes for cryptocurrency. It's a tool, and like any tool, its value lies in what it enables us to do.

Cryptocurrency promises freedom from bank fees, delays, and financial censorship. It promises a future where you have full control over your money, your data, and your destiny. It provides an opportunity to participate in a 24/7 international financial system that is unrestricted by geographical or political boundaries. For some, it's an investment; for others, a lifeline. For you? That's what we're here to explore.

In this book, we'll cover the basics: what cryptocurrency is, how it works, and why it's important. We'll look at the technology that powers it—blockchain—and explain how it provides security and transparency. We'll delve into popular cryptocurrencies like Bitcoin, Ethereum, and even some lesser-known players. We'll explore how cryptocurrency is being used today, from buying a cup of coffee to raising billions of dollars in capital. And we'll peek into the future to see where it all might be headed.

Before we journey further, a word of caution: the world of cryptocurrency is ever-changing. While this book offers a snapshot based on the most current data and trends, it's essential to stay updated on the latest news and shifts in this dynamic field.

Whether you're a complete beginner or looking to deepen your understanding, we've got something for you. So let's embark on this journey together. Fasten your seatbelt, secure your crypto wallet, and prepare to demystify the captivating world of cryptocurrency!

Who This Book Is For

This book is designed for a broad audience, whether you're just dipping your toes into the world of cryptocurrency or you're looking to build upon existing knowledge. Below are some of the groups who will find this book especially useful:

1. **Complete Beginners:** If terms like "blockchain" and "Bitcoin" are foreign to you, worry not. This book starts with the basics, making it easy for anyone to grasp the essential concepts.

2. **Casual Enthusiasts:** Maybe you've dabbled a bit in crypto or read a few articles. This book will deepen your understanding and provide you with a comprehensive view of the crypto world.
3. **Investors:** Whether you're considering your first cryptocurrency investment or looking to diversify your portfolio, this book offers practical advice on evaluation, risk management, and best practices.
4. **Professionals:** If you're in finance, law, or a related field, understanding cryptocurrency can be crucial as it becomes more integrated into these sectors.
5. **Tech-Savvy Individuals:** Those with a background in technology will find the deeper dives into blockchain and crypto architecture enlightening.
6. **Policy Makers and Regulators:** As cryptocurrency continues to gain traction, legal and regulatory challenges will follow. This book offers an overview that can aid in informed decision-making.
7. **The Simply Curious:** If you're here just to understand what all the buzz is about, you'll find that this book demystifies complex topics in a way that's engaging and easy to understand.

No matter your level of expertise or the reason for your interest, this book aims to be your comprehensive guide to all things crypto.

What You Will Learn

Let's delve into what specific skills and knowledge you can expect to acquire throughout the course of this book. Our objective is not just to offer facts, but also to empower you with the know-how to engage with the world of cryptocurrency intelligently and safely. Here's a glimpse of what lies ahead:

1. **Fundamental Concepts:** Learn the basics, from what a cryptocurrency is to how blockchain technology underpins it.
2. **Different Types of Cryptocurrencies:** Gain an understanding of the various kinds of digital currencies out there, beyond just Bitcoin and Ethereum.
3. **How to Buy and Store Cryptocurrency:** Understand how to navigate cryptocurrency exchanges, and how to secure your assets through digital wallets.
4. **Understanding Risks:** Get a grip on the kinds of risks involved in cryptocurrency investments, and how to mitigate them.
5. **Practical Usage:** Learn how cryptocurrencies are being used today, both in everyday transactions and as investment tools.
6. **Legal and Regulatory Landscape:** Acquaint yourself with the current state of cryptocurrency regulations and what it means for users and investors.
7. **Blockchain Technology:** A deeper dive into the architecture of blockchain, understanding why it's considered secure and how it could revolutionize various industries.
8. **Future Trends:** Get insights into where cryptocurrencies and blockchain technology might be headed in the coming years.
9. **Crypto in the Global Context:** Understand how cryptocurrency fits into the larger economic landscape, and what it means for global finance.
10. **Hands-On Activities:** Peppered throughout the book are practical exercises and activities to help solidify your understanding and provide real-world context.

By the end of this book, you'll be equipped with the foundational knowledge to intelligently discuss cryptocurrency, consider investments, and understand the potential impact of this technology on the world at large.

Part I: The Birth of Money and Currency

Section 1: Introduction to Money and Currency

Money has always been an integral part of human civilization, acting as the lifeblood that fuels the exchange of goods and services. From the early days of barter systems to the invention of physical currency, the concept of money has evolved in tandem with society. But what we're witnessing today is nothing short of revolutionary. In this section, we'll explore the very essence of what money is and how currency functions as a medium of exchange, a unit of account, and a store of value.

Yet, money is more than just coins and paper bills in your wallet; it's a concept that reflects the socio-economic structures we live in. It embodies trust, value, and a shared belief system among those who use it. We'll delve into the traditional financial systems that have been the cornerstone of economies worldwide, examining their strengths and vulnerabilities.

In a rapidly digitizing world, the digitalization of money was inevitable. As we transition from paper to digital, new questions arise: What is the role of banks in this new paradigm? How is the concept of value being redefined? And, most crucially, where does cryptocurrency fit into all this?

By understanding the fundamental principles of money and traditional currency, you'll be better equipped to grasp the transformative power of cryptocurrency. Whether you're a novice in the financial world or an expert looking for a refresher, this section will lay the foundation for the discussions that follow on cryptocurrencies and blockchain technology.

So let's delve in, shall we? A deeper understanding of money and currency will not only illuminate the path of financial history but also shed light on the exciting possibilities that lie ahead.

1.1 The Basics of Money

Ah, money. It's more than just paper and metal we exchange for goods and services. It's a story we've all bought into, a narrative that has evolved dramatically over the millennia. To really grasp the idea of cryptocurrencies, let's take a step back in time to understand the essence of money itself.

So, what is money? Fundamentally, it's a medium of exchange—a way for us to trade things without the awkwardness of barter. Imagine being a chicken farmer who needed to buy bread. Without money, you'd need to find a baker who just happened to want chickens. Not very efficient, right? So along came money, the great facilitator.

Coins made from precious metals were among the earliest forms of money. Why metals? They were durable, divisible, and had intrinsic value. Fast forward a bit, and we see the emergence of paper money, a promissory note that could be traded for gold or silver stored in a bank. Ah, but lugging around bags of coins was cumbersome and dangerous. Thus, the notes became valuable in their own right, leading to the birth of modern banking.

Fast forward to today, and money has gone digital. No, not crypto—yet! I'm talking about the numbers in your bank account, moving around the globe as electronic data. Quite a leap from bags of salt and metal coins, isn't it?

So, why does this history lesson matter? Because understanding what money has been will give us incredible insights into what money could be—our very own financial future represented by cryptocurrencies.

Keep these core principles in mind as we venture into the uncharted waters of digital currencies. If you can understand the origins and evolution of money, you'll find it much easier to wrap your head around the revolutionary concepts that cryptocurrencies bring to the table.

Now that we've laid the foundation, we're ready to dig into the good stuff. Buckle up! We're about to take a wild ride through the thrilling landscape of cryptocurrency.

1.2 The Evolution of Money

Imagine a world where every transaction requires a direct swap. You have a bushel of apples and you want a loaf of bread. You find someone who needs apples and has bread, and a trade is made. Simple, right? But what happens if you have apples and want a haircut? It could get messy.

This is the barter system, and while it seems quaint now, it was how people did business for thousands of years. It's like a never-ending game of "Go Fish," where you have to hope that someone else has exactly what you need. And it's as tedious as it sounds.

Then came the moment someone decided to introduce a middleman—a "thing," let's call it, that would represent value. We're talking about the first form of currency. Maybe it was seashells, or salt, or huge stone wheels if you lived on the island of Yap. Yes, you heard that right: stone wheels! In Yap, they use limestone discs called Rai stones as a form of currency. Some are as large as cars. Imagine lugging that around to pay for dinner.

So, currency made life easier but had its problems. For one, you had to carry it, whether it was metal coins, paper bills, or enormous stone wheels. Secondly, currencies were local. Your British pounds wouldn't do you any good in ancient China, where they used bronze shells.

Enter the digital age, and along comes cryptocurrency—money that's just a string of numbers and letters. There is no need to carry it, and no need to worry about exchange rates. It's borderless and instant. It's like we've circled back to the idea of trade, but with a digital twist.

So why is this important? Because understanding how we went from swapping apples to trading digital codes gives us a critical perspective. It helps us appreciate the revolutionary nature of cryptocurrency while also understanding that it's just the latest chapter in the epic tale of what we call money.

In this section, we'll investigate how the concept of currency has evolved, and ponder where it's headed next. We'll dig into the successes and the failures, the conveniences and the complications. Strap in—this historical joyride could give you a whole new outlook on your digital wallet!

1.3 Modern-Day Money

We're not dealing with barter systems or gold coins in pouches anymore. Today's money is often just a series of numbers on a computer screen. You might have a credit card in your wallet, but really, it's just a plastic gateway to those digits that represent your wealth—or debt. Heck, even the cash in your wallet is a stand-in for value, backed by nothing more than collective trust and legal systems.

What's fascinating about modern-day money is how intangible it has become. We've moved from physical trade goods to metal coins, from paper notes to digital currencies. Each step in this evolution has made money more convenient but also more abstract. It's a series of 1s and 0s on a computer somewhere, protected by layers of encryption and security measures.

In this shift, we've gained speed and efficiency. A transaction that once required a face-to-face meeting can now be done halfway around the world in a matter of seconds. But what have we given up? Some say it's a loss of a tangible connection to our wealth, a disconnect from the physicality that once defined trade and commerce.

In the chapters to follow, we'll explore the advantages and drawbacks of modern-day money, how it compares to historical forms of currency, and how digital cryptocurrencies aim to redefine what money is in the 21st century. So, if you're still hanging on to the notion that money is merely paper and coins, buckle up. You're in for an enlightening ride.

1.4 What is Currency?

Currency is more than just the paper bills and metal coins clinking in your pocket. It's the lifeblood of economies, the fuel for transactions, and the tangible representation of value in a society. But have you ever stopped to think about what currency actually is?

In essence, currency is a system of money that is accepted within a particular country or group of countries. It's what you use to pay for your groceries, what companies use to compensate their employees, and what governments use to collect taxes. Currency allows us to quantify the value of goods and services, making trade more straightforward and less prone to the pitfalls of bartering—like how many chickens are really equal to one cow?

Currencies come in various forms, each with its own set of rules and values. There are the well-known ones like the U.S. dollar, the Euro, and the British pound. Then there are digital currencies like Bitcoin, which don't exist in physical form but have value nonetheless. And let's not forget about community currencies, which are often used within a specific locality and are usually not legally recognized but still facilitate trade among members of a community.

What sets one type of currency apart from another is its range of acceptance and the stability of its value. The more stable and widely accepted a currency, the more likely it is to be used for both local and international transactions. That's why some currencies are considered 'hard' or 'strong,' making them preferred for international trade.

So, the next time you reach for your wallet, remember: currency is not just paper and metal; it's a complex system that reflects the economic and social structures of our world. Understanding this system is your first step toward grasping the even more complex and intriguing world of cryptocurrency.

1.5 Types of Currency

In a world as diverse as ours, it's no surprise that currencies are equally varied. Whether you're swapping digital numbers on a screen or handing over crumpled bills, you're participating in a system that has evolved over thousands of years. So let's take a moment to appreciate the different kinds of currency that circulate in economies around the world today.

Fiat Money

The term 'fiat' is derived from the Latin word that means "let it be done." This kind of currency has value because a government says it does. Most modern currencies, like the U.S. dollar or the Euro, are forms of fiat money. They're not backed by a physical commodity like gold; instead, their value is supported by the trust and confidence of the people who use them.

Commodity Money

Unlike fiat money, commodity money is backed by a physical good. In ancient times, this could have been anything from shells to salt. In more recent history, precious metals like gold and silver have been popular choices. The value of the currency is directly linked to the value of the commodity backing it, providing a tangible sense of security.

Cryptocurrency

Cryptocurrencies such as Bitcoin and Ethereum are examples of digital or virtual currencies and are the newest innovation in finance. They use cryptography for security and operate independently of a central authority. While they've garnered a lot of attention and speculation, they also offer innovative features like anonymity and decentralization.

Representative Money

Think of this as a placeholder for something else of value. Representative money itself doesn't hold intrinsic value but can be exchanged for a commodity. A good example is a gold certificate, where the paper itself isn't valuable, but it can be exchanged for a specific amount of gold.

Local and Community Currencies

Sometimes, smaller communities create their own currencies to encourage local trade and keep money circulating within the area. Examples include the Bristol Pound in the United Kingdom or BerkShares in Massachusetts, USA. These currencies usually coexist with national currencies but are used to support local businesses and foster community ties.

So there you have it—a whirlwind tour of the diverse world of currency. As we move forward, you'll see that understanding these basic types is crucial, especially when we delve into the disruptive influence of cryptocurrency on these traditional forms.

1.6 Transition from Physical to Digital Currency

The transition from physical to digital currency is like a tale of two cities—it brings with it the best and worst of times. On one hand, the digital evolution has made transactions more convenient, instantaneous, and global. On the other, it has raised new challenges that could make your head spin faster than a coin toss. Let's delve into some of these issues, shall we?

Problems with Physical Currency

1. **Wear and Tear:** Physical money gets old, torn, and damaged. The costs of printing new money and destroying the old can be a burden on a country's economy.
2. **Inconvenience:** Carrying around heaps of metal coins or wads of paper bills? Not the most convenient if you're buying a car or a house. And let's not get started on the hassle of making exact change.
3. **Security Risks:** Physical money can be stolen, lost, or counterfeit. You can't put a firewall around a wallet full of cash, and it doesn't come with password protection.

4. **Lack of Traceability:** Cash transactions are anonymous, which can be a benefit but also a significant downside. Anonymity makes it easier for illegal transactions to go unnoticed.

Problems with Digital Currency

   1. **Cybersecurity Risks:** Ah, the flip side of technological advancement. With great power comes great responsibility—and in this case, that means protecting yourself from hackers, scams, and fraud.
   2. **Accessibility:** Not everyone has a smartphone, a computer, or access to high-speed internet. The shift to digital currency can marginalize those who are not tech-savvy or lack the resources to participate.
   3. **Volatility:** Digital currencies, especially cryptocurrencies, can be notoriously unstable. A currency that can halve in value overnight is not for the faint of heart.
   4. **Regulatory and Compliance Issues:** The digital landscape is like the Wild West when it comes to regulations. Laws are still catching up, and that means navigating a confusing mishmash of rules and potential legal pitfalls.
   5. **Privacy Concerns:** Unlike cash transactions, digital ones leave a trail. How that data is used, stored, or potentially abused is a growing concern.

The move from physical to digital currency is a double-edged sword, offering tantalizing possibilities while presenting new challenges that society has yet to fully understand or address. As we inch closer to a cashless world, it's crucial to consider these factors. After all, every coin—physical or digital—has two sides.

The Double-Edged Sword of Convenience

First off, let's talk about convenience, because who doesn't like things to be easy? Digital currency lets you make payments with the swipe of a finger, whether you're sitting at home in your pajamas or traveling across international borders. The thought of tapping your phone to pay for a cup of coffee would have been laughable a couple of decades ago. But with this convenience comes a price—no pun intended.

The risk of cybersecurity breaches can't be understated. A single hack could compromise your financial details and leave your digital wallet as empty as a pirate's treasure chest after a mutiny. Just think of the major cybersecurity incidents that have taken place in recent years, from the Equifax data breach to ransomware attacks on major infrastructure. The point is, while digital currency is convenient, it is not entirely risk-free. You must be constantly vigilant, safeguarding your data like a hawk watching over its nest.

The Financial Divide

Let's not forget about accessibility. For all the hype about how digital currencies are the future, it's easy to overlook that not everyone has climbed aboard the digital bandwagon. In rural areas and developing nations, people still rely heavily on physical currency. A lack of technological infrastructure, combined with limited access to the internet, keeps them tethered to a cash-based ecosystem. As the world marches ahead, these communities risk being left behind, their economic possibilities stunted. Imagine being on the wrong side of a digital divide that has financial implications; it's a sobering thought.

Rolling the Dice with Volatility

Speaking of sobering thoughts, let's talk about the rollercoaster ride that is digital currency volatility. Cryptocurrencies are the poster child for financial fluctuations, sometimes swinging wildly in value within the span of hours or even minutes. Traditional fiat currencies also experience fluctuations, but they are generally more stable due to government backing and widespread usage. For those unprepared or unaware, engaging with volatile digital currencies can be akin to walking into a financial minefield with a blindfold on. So, if you're going to play the game, you better know the rules, and even then, brace yourself for a bumpy ride.

The Regulatory Labyrinth

It's tempting to view the digital landscape as a modern-day Wild West, a frontier ripe for exploration and exploitation. But as with any frontier, there's a need for law and order. Regulations exist, but they are often inconsistent and confusing, varying from one jurisdiction to another. Businesses accepting digital currency have to grapple with this regulatory patchwork, and the cost of compliance can be steep. What's more, the absence of a centralized authority makes it difficult to enforce rules and punish wrongdoers effectively.

Trading Privacy for Traceability

One could argue that digital currencies offer greater transparency because every transaction is recorded on a ledger. While that might sound like a benefit, it also means your financial activities are far less private. Your purchases, big or small, can be traced back to you, and that data can be used in ways you might not anticipate. What if insurance companies used your spending habits to assess your health risks? The notion that your financial activities could be scrutinized and used against you in some way is unsettling, to say the least.

The Final Word

The transition from physical to digital currency offers a glimpse into a future full of tantalizing possibilities. It promises to rewrite the rules of commerce, reshape how we interact with money, and redefine our financial identity. Yet, for every step forward, there are pitfalls that we must navigate carefully. As society inches ever closer to this new frontier, the conversation about its potential benefits and inherent risks will continue to evolve. But one thing is clear: the switch to digital currency is not just a financial evolution; it's a societal revolution that challenges us to reevaluate our relationship with money in ways we never thought possible. Like the pioneers of old, we're stepping into a new world, one filled with both promise and uncertainty. So as you buckle your seatbelt for this financial rollercoaster, remember that understanding the full picture—both the good and the bad—is essential for navigating the road ahead.

1.7 Key Takeaways

1. Money serves as a medium of exchange, a unit of account, and a store of value in our society.
2. The forms of money have evolved from barter systems to gold and silver coins, and eventually to paper currency and digital formats.
3. Modern-day money is often fiat currency, backed not by physical commodities but by trust in the issuing government.
4. Both physical and digital currencies have their advantages and drawbacks, from ease of use to risks like theft or inflation.
5. The transition from physical to digital currency has been accelerated by technological innovations but comes with its own set of challenges.
6. Understanding the history and functions of money and currency lays the foundation for grasping the revolutionary potential of cryptocurrencies.

Section 2: Traditional Financial Systems

In the landscape of money and finance, the traditional systems stand like ancient monuments—grand, complex, but not without their cracks and weathering. These are the institutions that have shaped the world we live in, the pillars on which modern economies stand. Banks, stock markets, and national currencies aren't just historical footnotes; they're living, breathing entities that affect our lives in tangible ways, for better or worse.

Yet, as pivotal as they are, these systems are not without their flaws—inequalities, inefficiencies, and the occasional collapse. Understanding them isn't just a lesson in history; it's crucial to grasping the full impact of the new kid on the block: cryptocurrency. This isn't a tale of David versus Goliath, but rather an intricate narrative of evolution and potential revolution.

In this section, we'll dissect the layers of traditional financial systems. We'll explore the origin of banks, the abstraction of credit, and even touch upon the governments that back (or sometimes destabilize) these financial mechanisms. This is important groundwork because, to fully comprehend why cryptocurrencies like Bitcoin and Ethereum matter, you have to understand what they're challenging.

So, with a discerning eye, let's examine these longstanding systems—both their strengths and their weaknesses. As we peel back the layers, we'll set the stage for the radical alternatives that cryptocurrencies offer.

2.1 Banks and Financial Institutions

Banks: monoliths of marble and stone, imposing yet familiar. These are the fortresses where our money sleeps, shielded by vaults and guarded by complex layers of security. But have you ever paused to ponder why banks exist? What is it about human society that birthed the need for these massive institutions of finance?

In the simplest terms, banks are the keepers of our money. They hold the savings of millions, administer loans, and facilitate transactions that keep the cogs of the economy turning. But it's more than mere storage and accounting; it's a deeply entrenched system of trust—or at least it used to be. For as long as human history can trace, people have sought secure places for their wealth, whether that be grain, precious metals, or digits on a computer screen. Banks evolved to fill this role, sanctioned and overseen by governments to ensure a semblance of reliability.

Yet, the system is far from perfect. Banks are centralized, top-down institutions, the antithesis of the decentralized philosophy that underscores cryptocurrencies. The centralized nature of banks makes them vulnerable to a myriad of risks: fraud, mismanagement, even outright collapse. Remember the financial crisis of 2008? That's a sobering testament to the fallibility of the banking system. Even if you didn't feel the tremors yourself, the aftermath rippled through the world economy like a financial earthquake, leaving no one untouched.

And let's not forget the 'unbanked,' a term used to describe the nearly two billion people who lack access to essential financial services. For them, the grandiose edifices of banking are like walled cities—unreachable and impenetrable. So, while banks may provide a sense of security and normalcy for many, they simultaneously exclude vast populations from the benefits that many take for granted.

In this subsection, we've peeled back the façade of banks to reveal not just their might, but also their frailties. Understanding these dynamics is critical as we move forward, for the story of cryptocurrency is, in part, a response to the limitations of traditional financial institutions. It's an echo of voices asking, "Isn't there a better way?"

As we proceed, remember that banks aren't just the backdrops of our financial lives; they are the stage on which the drama of cryptocurrency is unfolding. With this foundational knowledge, we'll delve deeper into the complexities and intricacies of traditional financial systems.

2.2 The Stock Market

The stock market is like the pulse of capitalism, a complex system that seems chaotic but follows certain rules—rules that can make or break fortunes. It's a marketplace, yes, but not for buying milk and bread. Here, people trade pieces of companies as if they're trading playing cards. The high stakes and rapid action might make it look like gambling, but don't be fooled; this is serious business, and there are many players involved, each with their own strategies and agendas.

From Wall Street to Tokyo's financial district, stock markets represent a key element of the traditional financial system. They're where companies go public, issuing shares that you and I can buy. The price of these shares can fluctuate based on a myriad of factors—everything from the company's latest earnings report to the overall mood of the market.

Investing in the stock market has long been a path to financial freedom, but it comes with its own risks and requires a certain level of knowledge. Unlike putting your money in a savings account, you're taking a risk when you invest in stocks. Yet, it's that very risk that makes it possible to earn a much higher return on your investment.

In this subsection, we'll explore the origins of stock markets, the mechanics of trading, and the role they play in modern-day economics. We'll look into things like Initial Public Offerings (IPOs), market indices like the S&P 500, and delve into some strategies that traders employ to try to beat the market.

High-frequency trading, bear and bull markets, short selling—it's like an entirely different language. But don't worry, by the end of this section, you'll be conversing fluently. Understanding the stock market is essential because it's a part of the broader financial system that directly or indirectly affects all of us.

So sit tight, as we're about to dive into a world that can be as rewarding as it is ruthless. Whether you're interested in investing or just curious about how this intricate system operates, the stock market is a subject that can't be ignored when discussing traditional financial systems.

2.3 Government and Money

If the stock market is the pulse of capitalism, then the government serves as its guiding hand. Think of it as the referee in a high-stakes game, setting the rules, keeping the peace, but also influencing the outcome. Governments don't just print money and control its flow; they have a direct impact on almost every facet of the financial system.

Throughout history, governments have sought to control money supply and manipulate currencies for various ends. They set interest rates, issue bonds, and control fiscal policy. These actions don't just sound important—they are. They can dictate the health of an economy, spur growth, or lead to financial ruin if mismanaged.

Ever heard of 'quantitative easing' or 'inflation targeting'? These aren't just buzzwords; they're strategies employed by central banks to stabilize or stimulate their country's economy. Governments can increase or decrease the money supply, often through a central bank like the Federal Reserve in the United States. They decide whether to make money cheap to borrow, encouraging investment and spending, or make it expensive to rein in an overheating economy.

But the government's role isn't confined to these big-picture strategies. It also regulates banks, stock markets, and other financial institutions to prevent fraud and protect consumers. After all, it was the lack of oversight that contributed to the 2008 financial crisis, a grim lesson that still looms large.

At the intersection of politics and economics, we find a tangle of policies and decisions that can seem overwhelming. But it's crucial to grasp how government involvement in the financial system is a double-edged sword—capable of both boosting and stifling economic growth.

So, whether you like it or not, the government is a player in the financial arena—one with a lot of power. Understanding its role is crucial to understanding the financial system we're all a part of. In the coming pages, we'll dissect these governmental powers and responsibilities, and examine how they affect you, the individual, navigating through this complex world.

2.4 Problems with Traditional Systems

Traditional financial systems, for all their benefits, are not without flaws. Think of them as old bridges—functional, yes, but in need of modernization. For starters, consider the concept of fees. Banks have mastered the art of nickel-and-diming customers for every service imaginable: wire transfers, overdrafts, monthly account maintenance. Sure, these fees are often considered the cost of doing business, but the cumulative impact on consumers can be staggering.

Another thorn in the side of traditional finance is accessibility. Not everyone has the privilege of walking into a bank to open an account. In many parts of the world, especially rural areas, banking services are limited or non-existent. Then there's the question of credit. Who gets it and who doesn't is often a decision made behind closed doors, based on a system that many believe is opaque and unfair.

Let's not forget about speed—or rather, the lack thereof. Transactions, especially international ones, can take days to clear. In a world where instant communication is the norm, waiting several days for a financial transaction to complete seems archaic.

And speaking of international transactions, the issue of currency conversion is yet another hurdle. The traditional financial system operates in a patchwork of currencies, all of which need to be exchanged, often at rates unfavorable to the consumer and with yet more fees attached.

Lastly, but certainly not least, is the issue of security. Traditional financial systems are susceptible to a variety of risks, including fraud, cyberattacks, and even the occasional bank failure. While systems have been put in place to mitigate these risks, the incidents are frequent enough to warrant concern.

All these problems create friction, inefficiency, and inequality in a system that's supposed to serve everyone equally. It's a maze of complications and barriers that has left many wondering if there's a better way. As we navigate through the nuances of these issues, we'll set the stage for the revolutionary solutions offered by cryptocurrencies. Stay tuned.

2.5 Key Takeaways

1. Traditional financial systems, while functional, are plagued with various problems like fees, accessibility issues, and slow transaction times.
2. The question of who gets access to credit in traditional systems is often opaque and considered unfair by many.
3. Speed is a significant drawback, with some international transactions taking days to complete.
4. Currency conversion in a multi-currency world is another obstacle, often laden with unfavorable rates and extra fees.
5. Security risks, such as fraud and cyberattacks, remain a constant concern in traditional financial settings.
6. These issues create inefficiencies and inequalities, setting the stage for the alternatives presented by the world of cryptocurrency.

Part II: The World of Bitcoin and Cryptocurrencies

Section 3: What is a Cryptocurrency?

The landscape of money is changing, and it's more than just a fresh coat of paint on an old house. We're talking a full-on architectural upheaval. As we journey deeper into the world of finance, it's time to shift our gaze to cryptocurrency—a radical newcomer with ambitions that stretch far beyond mere bells and whistles.

It's a term that's been thrown around like a hot potato in financial circles. But what does it really mean? What challenges does it pose to the status quo, and what answers might it offer to the age-old problems we've been wrestling with? Before we throw ourselves into these complex waters, let's set the stage. This section is your guidepost, your primer into the world of digital wallets and decentralized finance.

Cryptocurrency isn't just a footnote in the financial story; it's shaping up to be its own epic saga. It aims to challenge—and perhaps even topple—the traditional pillars we've just explored. Here, we'll demystify the technology, explore its potential, and wrestle with its implications.

It's not simple; revolutions rarely are. And this section is where we confront the meat of the matter. Ready? Good. It's time to tear away the curtain and examine the machine at work. We're diving into the knitty-gritty of what cryptocurrency really is, why it matters, and how it could change our financial lives forever. Buckle up.

3.1 Definition and Origin

Let's start with basics, shall we? What, exactly, is cryptocurrency? The term itself is a mash-up of "cryptography," the art of writing and solving codes, and "currency," a system of money. But that's just skimming the surface. A cryptocurrency is digital or virtual money that relies on cryptography for security. There are no physical coins or bills. Everything happens online.

This didn't just appear out of thin air. It has a starting point, and that point is named Bitcoin. Created by an anonymous figure known as Satoshi Nakamoto in 2009, Bitcoin was the world's first cryptocurrency. It emerged in the aftermath of the 2008 financial crisis, a tumultuous period that shook the traditional financial system to its core. Many saw it as a solution to the flaws and vulnerabilities that the crisis had laid bare.

Bitcoin was engineered to be a decentralized system. That means no single entity, like a bank or government, has control over it. Transactions are verified by a network of people—often called miners—and recorded in a public ledger known as a blockchain. We'll get into the details of blockchain later, but for now, just know that it's a technology that enables secure, transparent transactions.

Since the birth of Bitcoin, the world has seen the rise of thousands of other cryptocurrencies, each with their own unique features and purposes. Some aim to be digital gold; others aim to facilitate smart contracts or fuel decentralized applications.

Why does this all matter? Because cryptocurrency challenges the very definition of what we consider money. It's not just a new way to pay for stuff; it's a rethinking of how financial transactions should be conducted, who should control them, and how they should be recorded.

This chapter is our gateway into understanding this groundbreaking shift. We're setting the stage, presenting the characters, and preparing you for the twists and turns that lie ahead. Cryptocurrency isn't just another chapter in the history of money; for some, it's a whole new book. So turn the page, and let's see where this story takes us.

3.2 How It Differs from Traditional Currency

In the grand tapestry of finance, cryptocurrency appears as a stark contrast to traditional forms of money. It's like comparing a typewriter to a laptop: both serve the same fundamental purpose, but the latter introduces functionalities and flexibilities that redefine the game.

First off, let's talk about control. In traditional financial systems, banks and governments are the stewards of currency. They regulate its value, control its supply, and act as intermediaries for transactions. Cryptocurrency, however, is a child of the internet, born of algorithms and maintained by a decentralized network of computers. No kings or captains here; it's a ship without a captain that still manages to navigate the waters.

The elimination of intermediaries brings us to our second point: speed and cost. Traditional transactions, especially across borders, can be slow and costly. Banks need their cut, and international rules need to be adhered to. But in the crypto world, transactions can happen in the blink of an eye, at any time, to any place around the globe, often at a fraction of the cost.

Then there's the issue of transparency and security. Ever tried tracing a dollar bill? It's almost impossible. The same can't be said for cryptocurrencies. Thanks to the blockchain, every transaction is recorded in a public ledger that anyone can view. While the identities of the people involved are encrypted, the details of the transaction itself are open for verification. It's a layer of accountability that traditional money simply lacks.

Finally, let's talk about accessibility. To participate in the traditional financial system, you need access to banks or financial institutions. This is a hurdle for billions of people around the world who are unbanked or underbanked. Cryptocurrency, being a product of the internet, is accessible to anyone with an internet connection. It's a financial system that doesn't discriminate based on geography or socioeconomic status.

The implications of these differences are immense. We're not just talking about a new kind of money; we're talking about a reimagining of financial systems and power structures. It's akin to the seismic shifts that accompanied the rise of the internet or the spread of mobile phones—technological advances that fundamentally changed how we live, work, and interact. Cryptocurrency, in its own unique way, is poised to do the same.

3.3 Key Takeaways

1. Cryptocurrency operates on a decentralized network, freeing it from the control of banks and governments.
2. The elimination of intermediaries in crypto transactions leads to faster speeds and often lower costs.
3. Unlike traditional money, every crypto transaction is publicly recorded on a blockchain, adding layers of transparency and security.
4. Cryptocurrency is accessible to anyone with an internet connection, breaking down barriers that exist in traditional financial systems.
5. The fundamental differences between traditional currency and cryptocurrency have the potential to reshape our financial systems and power structures.
6. Cryptocurrency isn't merely a new form of money; it's a technological revolution with wide-reaching implications.

Section 4: Introduction to Bitcoin

Let's set the stage. The year is 2008, and someone, or maybe a group of people, under the name Satoshi Nakamoto has just dropped something huge—a new kind of money called Bitcoin. Imagine someone scribbling an idea on a napkin, an idea that would shake up how we think about money, but doing it anonymously, like a masked hero. That's Bitcoin for you—a game-changer in disguise.

So why should you care about Bitcoin? Well, it's like the first chapter in a much larger story, one that we're all a part of. It's the first domino that fell, setting off a chain reaction leading to a whole world of cryptocurrencies. And like the first chapter of any great story, you've got to understand it to make sense of everything that follows.

This isn't just history, folks. Bitcoin is very much alive and kicking. In this section, we'll dive deep into what makes Bitcoin, well, Bitcoin. We'll look at how it came to be and why it matters. So as we unravel the tale of this digital coin, let's pay attention to the bigger questions it raises—questions about who's in charge of our money and what freedom really means.

So, are you ready to unmask the mysterious Bitcoin? Let's get started.

4.1 What is Bitcoin and how does it work?

Imagine a kind of money that's not a paper bill or a metal coin, but something you can only see on a computer screen. That's Bitcoin. It's like the money you use to buy a snack or a toy, except it lives purely in the digital world. There's no bank controlling it, no government printing it, and no one can tell you how to use it. You've got the power—pretty neat, huh?

But how does it work? Good question. The magic—or let's say the genius—behind Bitcoin is a kind of online ledger called a "blockchain." Picture a big notebook that everyone can see, but no one can cheat or erase what's written in it. Every time someone sends or receives Bitcoin, that transaction gets written in this notebook for all to see. This keeps everyone honest.

To make a Bitcoin transaction, you need two things: a public key and a private key. Think of the public key like your email address—something you give people so they can send you Bitcoin. The private key? That's like your secret password, something you keep safe and never share, because it allows you to send Bitcoin to others.

But let's not forget miners—the people who make the whole thing tick. They're the ones who verify the transactions, making sure no one is cheating. For their hard work, they get some newly minted Bitcoin. It's like a reward for being the referees in this game of digital money.

Now, you may be wondering about the value of Bitcoin. Well, it's a rollercoaster. Sometimes it's up, sometimes it's down, and that makes it both exciting and risky. But one thing's for sure: it's captured the world's attention, and it's making us rethink what money can be.

In this section, we're going to dig deeper into the creases and folds of this fascinating digital currency. From its mysterious origins to how it's shaking up the financial world, we'll pull back the curtain and let you in on the secrets. So tighten your seatbelt, because we're diving into the world of Bitcoin.

4.2 Brief History and Its Creator

Let's take a step back in time to 2008. The world was a bit shaky. Banks were failing, and trust in traditional money was at an all-time low. Then, out of the shadows, an anonymous figure—or maybe even a group of people—named Satoshi Nakamoto dropped a bombshell. This person, or these people, published a paper explaining a new kind of money called Bitcoin.

Satoshi's idea was radical. Create a digital currency that doesn't rely on banks or governments, a currency that people could trade directly with each other. This was like inventing a new kind of wheel, one that could roll on its own without any help.

So what happened next? Well, in 2009, the first Bitcoin transaction took place. Slowly but surely, more people started taking notice. It was like a snowball rolling down a hill, gathering more snow and getting bigger with each turn.

Fast-forward to today, and Bitcoin has become a household name. Satoshi Nakamoto, however, remains a mystery. Despite countless attempts to reveal the identity, or identities, of this enigmatic creator, we're still in the dark. Some say it's a single genius; others speculate it might be a group of brilliant minds. The truth? We don't know, and maybe we never will.

The anonymity of Satoshi adds an extra layer of intrigue to Bitcoin. It's like a modern-day legend, full of mystique and fascination. But regardless of who created it, one thing is certain: Bitcoin has left an indelible mark on how we think about money.

We'll delve deeper into the nuances and turning points in Bitcoin's history, but for now, just know this: It started as an idea—a revolutionary one—and has turned into something the whole world is talking about. So let's explore this extraordinary story together.

4.3 Bitcoin Mining

You might have heard the term "Bitcoin mining" and wondered what it has to do with digital money. No, it's not about pickaxes and underground tunnels. This is a different kind of mining, one that takes place in the realm of computers and complex calculations. But just like traditional mining seeks valuable minerals, Bitcoin mining seeks something equally valuable: new Bitcoins.

Let's break it down. The Bitcoin network relies on a public ledger called the blockchain. Think of it as a giant, unchangeable notebook that keeps a record of every single Bitcoin transaction. But for this notebook to stay accurate and secure, someone has to do the math—lots and lots of math.

Enter the miners. These are people with specialized computers designed to solve complicated puzzles. When they solve one, they get to add a new "block" of transactions to the blockchain. This is crucial because adding this block confirms and secures every transaction within it.

Now, the system doesn't just take their word for it. The other miners have to agree that the math checks out. It's a bit like having a team of accountants double-checking each other's work. Once everyone agrees, the new block is added, and the successful miner gets a reward: new Bitcoins, fresh from the digital press. This is how new Bitcoins are born.

But there's a catch. These puzzles get more complicated over time, requiring more computing power. It's as if the Bitcoin network keeps raising the bar, making it harder to earn those coveted new Bitcoins. Some say it's to keep the system secure; others argue it's an energy drain, consuming as much electricity as some small countries.

So why do miners put up with all this trouble? Simple. The reward is often worth the effort. At various points in its history, a single Bitcoin has been worth thousands, even tens of thousands, of dollars. Imagine being the miner who unlocks that treasure.

Bitcoin mining is an intricate, vital part of the Bitcoin ecosystem. It's what keeps the system ticking, ensuring transactions are secure and new Bitcoins continue to be generated. However, it's also a subject of controversy, a complex puzzle in itself that we'll explore more as we go along. So hold onto your hats, the journey into the belly of the Bitcoin beast is just getting started.

4.4 Use-Cases for Bitcoin

You might be thinking, "Okay, Bitcoin sounds cool, but what can I actually do with it?" Great question. At first glance, Bitcoin might seem like a mysterious coin from a digital treasure chest. But it's far more than that. Bitcoin has real-world applications—ways you can use it—that are changing the game in everything from shopping to sending money across the globe.

Let's start with something basic: buying stuff. Yes, you can use Bitcoin to buy things, both online and, in some cases, even in physical stores. There's a growing list of businesses that accept Bitcoin for all sorts of goods, from computer parts to, believe it or not, pizza. The process is straightforward: you send Bitcoin from your digital wallet to the seller's wallet, just like you would hand over cash or swipe a credit card.

Speaking of credit cards, you know those annoying fees you have to pay when you use one? With Bitcoin, those can be significantly lower or sometimes even nonexistent. That's a major plus for both buyers and sellers.

But Bitcoin isn't just for shopping. It's also a favorite for international transactions. If you've ever had to send money overseas, you know it can be a hassle. Fees are high, and it can take days for the transaction to go through. With Bitcoin, you can send money anywhere in the world, almost instantly, and for a fraction of the usual cost.

And let's not forget about investments. Many people buy Bitcoins hoping that the value will go up over time, similar to how you might invest in stocks or real estate. It's a risky game, sure. Bitcoin's value has been known to swing wildly, but the potential for high returns has made it an attractive option for some investors.

However, it's not all sunshine and rainbows. Bitcoin has its darker sides too. Its anonymity features have made it a popular choice for illegal activities, including money laundering and purchasing illegal goods. This has attracted the attention of governments and regulators, who are still figuring out how to deal with these challenges.

So, what's the verdict? Bitcoin is a versatile tool, capable of much more than just sitting pretty in a digital wallet. It offers a new way to shop, invest, and transfer money worldwide. But like any tool, it comes with its risks and controversies. It's a pioneering force, breaking new ground and setting the stage for what could be the future of finance. But, as with any frontier, there are obstacles, uncertainties, and even dangers along the way. Keep that in mind as we delve deeper into the evolving world of Bitcoin.

4.5 Bitcoin Storage Options

Alright, let's say you've got your hands on some Bitcoin. Maybe you mined it yourself, or perhaps you bought some as an investment.

Either way, you've got a digital treasure on your hands. So, where do you keep it? Unlike the money in your wallet or the coins in your piggy bank, storing Bitcoin requires a bit of know-how.

The place where you keep your Bitcoin is called a "wallet," but don't let that term fool you. It's not a physical thing; it's a piece of software that keeps track of your Bitcoin transactions. And there are different types of wallets, each with its own set of pros and cons.

First up, there's the online wallet, which you can access from anywhere with an internet connection. Sounds convenient, right? Well, it is, but there's a catch. Because it's online, it's susceptible to hacking. You've probably heard stories of people losing their Bitcoin to cybercriminals; this is often how it happens.

Then, you have desktop wallets. These are software programs you download onto your computer. They offer a bit more security than online wallets, but if your computer gets a virus or crashes, you could still lose everything. You'd better have some solid anti-virus software and regular backups if you go this route.

If you're looking for something even more secure, consider a hardware wallet. It's a physical device, almost like a tiny computer, that stores your Bitcoin offline. Even if someone hacks into your regular computer, they won't be able to get to the Bitcoin on your hardware wallet unless they physically have the device.

Lastly, there's the paper wallet. Yes, you read that right—paper. Your Bitcoin information is printed out and kept in a physical form. It's completely offline, making it highly secure against hacking. But if you lose that piece of paper, or if it gets damaged, your Bitcoin is gone. So you'd better have a safe place to keep it.

Each type of wallet comes with its own set of challenges and considerations. Online wallets are convenient but risky. Desktop wallets offer more control but require vigilance. Hardware wallets are secure but can be expensive. Paper wallets are impenetrable but also fragile.

So there you have it—the ins and outs of Bitcoin storage. Each option has its own share of risks and rewards, and the best choice depends on your needs, your technical know-how, and how much risk you're willing to take. It's like choosing a safe for your family jewels—you need to weigh your options carefully. Because in the digital age, where hacking is a real and present danger, where you store your Bitcoin is nearly as important as owning it in the first place.

4.6 Key Takeaways

1. Storing Bitcoin requires a digital "wallet," which isn't a physical object but rather a software program that tracks your cryptocurrency transactions.
2. There are several types of wallets: online, desktop, hardware, and paper, each with its own set of advantages and disadvantages.
3. Online wallets are convenient but vulnerable to hacking. Desktop wallets offer more control but require regular maintenance and backups.
4. Hardware wallets offer the highest level of security by keeping your Bitcoin offline, but they can be a bit pricey.
5. Paper wallets are ultra-secure but risky if you lose or damage the paper.
6. The best wallet for you depends on your specific needs and how much risk you're willing to take. Choose wisely, as the safety of your Bitcoin is at stake.

Section 5: Beyond Bitcoin - Altcoins, Tokens, NFTs

By now, you've learned quite a bit about Bitcoin, the pioneer that kicked off the cryptocurrency revolution. But let's not forget, Bitcoin isn't the only game in town. Imagine walking into a digital playground filled with a multitude of activities. Sure, the towering slide at the center—that's Bitcoin—grabs your immediate attention. But what about the swings, the merry-go-round, and the jungle gym? They may not be as high or as grand, but they're equally fun and unique in their own ways.

That's the world of cryptocurrency for you. It's brimming with options beyond Bitcoin—some made to solve its flaws, others born from entirely different ideas and needs. These are known as altcoins (alternative coins), tokens, and NFTs (Non-Fungible Tokens). Don't worry; these terms might sound like they come straight out of a science fiction novel, but we're going to break them down for you.

Altcoins can be thought of as cousins to Bitcoin. Created using the same basic DNA—blockchain technology—these coins aim to fill in the gaps where Bitcoin might fall short. Some offer quicker transactions, others promise total anonymity, and a few even cater to specific online communities.

Then there are tokens. Imagine you're at a fair. You exchange your dollars for tokens to ride the Ferris wheel or grab some cotton candy. In the digital world, tokens work similarly, but they offer a lot more than rides and treats. Tokens are specialized units created on existing blockchains and are often designed for a particular online community, service, or application.

Last but not least, we have NFTs, or Non-Fungible Tokens. In a way, these are the collector's items of the digital realm. Think of owning an autographed baseball card, but instead of paper and ink, it's bits and bytes stored securely on a blockchain. And it's not just cards; it can be digital art, online real estate, or even a tweet. What makes NFTs special is that each one is unique, like a fingerprint or a snowflake.

So why do these alternatives to Bitcoin matter? Each one serves a different purpose and appeals to various needs and desires. They expand the world of digital finance, opening doors to possibilities that we're only beginning to imagine. By understanding them, you're not just getting a complete picture of the crypto landscape; you're also unlocking new avenues for investment, application, and innovation.

We'll explore each of these digital wonders in the coming subsections. You'll learn what sets them apart, how they're created, and what they're used for. And we'll also get into why some people think they're the future of everything from online buying and selling to digital art collecting.

But remember, the crypto world is ever-changing. New altcoins, tokens, and NFTs are being created all the time, while others fade away. It's like an ongoing treasure hunt, and you never know what you might find next. So keep your eyes open and your mind ready to explore. This section is going to be a ride—a ride on a digital merry-go-round where each horse is different, and every turn brings a new thrill. Let's dive in.

5.1 What Are Altcoins?

So, we've been talking a lot about Bitcoin, right? But let me tell you, that's just the tip of the iceberg. Imagine if the only car you ever knew was a Ford Model T. Sure, it's a classic, a real game-changer. But then, one day, you walk into a modern car showroom, and your eyes widen. There's not just one type of car; there are dozens! Sedans,

SUVs, electric cars, and more. Each with their own bells and whistles, built to solve different problems and meet various needs.

That's exactly what altcoins are to Bitcoin. They're the Toyotas, Teslas, and Jeeps of the cryptocurrency world. The term "altcoin" is short for "alternative coin," which means they're different versions of the original Bitcoin. Many of them are built using similar technology but tweaked to offer something that Bitcoin doesn't.

You might be wondering, "Why do we need other types of cryptocurrency if we already have Bitcoin?" Well, think about why there's more than one type of car. Some people need something fast and sporty; others might want something that's good for the environment. It's the same with altcoins; they were made to fill in the gaps where Bitcoin might not be the perfect fit.

So, what makes altcoins different from Bitcoin? Let's break it down into a few key areas:

Speed and Scalability

Bitcoin is like the granddaddy of cryptocurrencies, but it's not exactly the fastest. Transactions can take longer to process compared to some newer cryptocurrencies. That's like waiting in line for a roller coaster—exciting but sometimes slow. Altcoins like Litecoin were designed to solve this problem, offering quicker transaction times.

Anonymity

While Bitcoin offers a level of privacy, it's not entirely anonymous. Imagine if you were reading a secret note in class, and your teacher could see the paper but not what's written on it. Some altcoins, like Monero, aim for complete anonymity, keeping both the note and the writing invisible.

Specific Use Cases

Some altcoins are like specialized tools in a toolbox, designed for very specific tasks. Take Ethereum, for example. It's not just a currency but a platform where people can build all sorts of applications, from games to smart contracts. It's like a Swiss Army knife in the crypto world.

Community Focus

A few altcoins aim to build a sense of community or support a cause. Dogecoin started as a joke but has become a symbol of internet culture and goodwill. It's like the class clown who ends up winning the school election.

Environmental Concerns

One of the criticisms of Bitcoin is that it consumes a lot of energy, just like some older models of cars aren't very fuel-efficient. Some altcoins, like Cardano, are looking to solve this issue by using different methods to verify transactions, which are less harmful to the planet.

You see, the world of altcoins is as diverse as it is large. There are over 11,000 different altcoins, according to some counts! They range from the serious and groundbreaking to the downright strange. For example, there's even a coin named after garlic bread—yes, you read that right, garlic bread!

Now, before you jump into the altcoin pool, it's good to remember that not all that glitters is gold. While some altcoins have groundbreaking potential, others might be what people call "pump and dump" schemes. These are coins that get a lot of hype and investment initially but quickly lose value. It's like buying a shiny new toy that breaks within a week. So, it's crucial to do your homework before diving in.

But why should you care about altcoins? Well, they're shaping the future of digital finance and technology. They're like the upcoming chapters in a book that's still being written, pushing the boundaries and exploring new possibilities. By understanding them, you're not just learning about alternative currencies; you're getting insights into how our world might look in the years to come.

So, the next time someone talks to you about cryptocurrency and mentions Bitcoin, you can nod and say, "Sure, but have you heard of altcoins?" Because now you know, Bitcoin is just the start, and the world of altcoins is like an open road, full of turns, twists, and endless possibilities.

Let's keep digging into this fascinating world. Up next, we'll dive into tokens and learn how they differ from coins, adding another layer to our growing knowledge of cryptocurrency. Stay tuned!

5.2 Notable Altcoins

Alright, so you've got a good grip on what altcoins are and why they're more than just Bitcoin's sidekicks. But with thousands of them out there, how do you know which ones are worth paying attention to? In this section, we'll zoom in on some of the standout stars in the altcoin universe: Ethereum, Ripple (XRP), Litecoin, and a few others that have made waves in the crypto sea. Think of them as the varsity team of the altcoin world, each with its own set of skills and game-changing moves. So, buckle up as we delve into the unique traits and groundbreaking contributions of these notable altcoins.

Ethereum

When people talk about Ethereum, they often describe it as the "younger sibling" to Bitcoin. But that's a bit like calling the Wright

Brothers' plane a younger sibling to a bicycle. Sure, they both involve wheels and get you places, but one of them can fly.

So, what's the big deal about Ethereum? Created in 2015 by a whiz kid named Vitalik Buterin, Ethereum took the blockchain technology that makes Bitcoin secure and transparent and asked, "What else can we do with this?" It turns out, the answer is a lot.

Picture blockchain like a digital notebook. Bitcoin uses it to keep track of who owns how much Bitcoin. Pretty straightforward, right? But Ethereum turned that digital notebook into a full-blown interactive journal where you can not only jot down who owns what, but also write mini-programs, known as "smart contracts," that can execute tasks automatically. You might be wondering what a "smart contract" is. Well, imagine a vending machine. You put in a dollar, and you get a candy bar. No need for a shopkeeper or a cashier. A smart contract works similarly but in the digital world. It's a set of rules that automatically do something when conditions are met, like transferring money or ownership of digital items.

This might sound like techy stuff, and it is. But it has some pretty down-to-earth uses, too. For example, with Ethereum's smart contracts, you could have an online garage sale where people buy your old stuff without you having to be there to collect the money. Once they pay the set price, the ownership transfers automatically. It's like having a self-running lemonade stand that never takes a day off.

Because of this smart contract feature, Ethereum has become the backbone for countless other projects in the crypto world. Companies have built applications for everything from trading virtual real estate to running entire businesses on the Ethereum platform. Think about that for a second: an entire business running on a digital platform, with no office space, no utility bills, and fewer middlemen. It's like a futuristic movie, but it's happening right now.

But, of course, there's a flip side. Remember, no technology is perfect. The more complex something is, the more chances there are for something to go wrong. Ethereum has had its share of bugs and security issues, some of which led to significant losses of money. People are still figuring out the best ways to secure these smart contracts, but the stakes are high. It's a bit like learning to fly a plane while already in the air.

Another issue is the environmental impact. Like Bitcoin, Ethereum uses a lot of electricity to keep its network secure and running smoothly. There are plans to make it more eco-friendly, but that's a work in progress. So, if you're someone who cares deeply about the planet, that's something to keep in mind.

Now, what about Ethereum as an investment? You've probably heard stories about people becoming overnight millionaires by investing in cryptocurrency. And while it's true that Ethereum's value has soared since its creation, investing in it comes with risks. The value of Ethereum, like any cryptocurrency, can go up but can also plunge down—sometimes very suddenly. So, if you're thinking about investing, remember the golden rule: never invest more than you can afford to lose.

In the end, Ethereum isn't just Bitcoin's "younger sibling." It's a revolutionary platform that's enabling new kinds of digital interactions and paving the way for what's being called the "decentralized web," where users have more control and ownership of their data. And whether you're a tech enthusiast or just a curious observer, Ethereum is a landmark in the ever-changing landscape of digital currency and technology.

To sum it up, Ethereum has made a significant impact in the short time it's been around. From introducing smart contracts to serving as a launchpad for other crypto projects, it's far more than just another digital currency. However, with great innovation comes great challenges, from security concerns to environmental questions. So, as we watch Ethereum and similar technologies unfold, it's essential to approach them with a balanced perspective, aware of both their groundbreaking potential and their limitations.

Ripple (XRP)

You've probably heard the phrase, "Don't put all your eggs in one basket." Well, in the world of cryptocurrencies, many people have done just that by investing only in Bitcoin or Ethereum. But there's another player on the block(chain) that's worth paying attention to—Ripple, or as you'll often see it referred to, XRP.

First things first: let's clear up some confusion. Ripple is the name of the company, and XRP is the cryptocurrency they developed. Imagine if a company named "Fruit" made a phone called the "Apple." You'd need to keep them straight, right? The same goes for Ripple and XRP.

So, what makes Ripple stand out in the crowded crypto space? The answer lies in its reason for being, which is a bit different from Bitcoin or Ethereum. While those cryptocurrencies aim to be a type of digital gold or a platform for smart contracts, Ripple targets a more specific problem: making it quicker and less costly to send money around the world. In short, it's about revolutionizing how we move money from Point A to Point B, especially when those points are in different countries.

Let's paint a picture. Imagine you have a cousin in another country, and she urgently needs some money for a medical bill. Traditional ways to send money across borders can be sluggish and expensive. We're talking days to complete and fees that could buy you a decent meal. Ripple aims to solve this by making the whole process almost instant and reducing the fees to a fraction of what they currently are.

How does it do this? Ripple uses XRP as a kind of "bridge" currency. Let's say you're sending dollars, and your cousin needs euros. Instead of converting dollars to euros, which can be slow and costly, you convert dollars to XRP and then XRP to euros. All of this happens in a matter of seconds. It's like having a super-efficient translator who can instantly translate your English words into any other language.

Of course, every rose has its thorns, and Ripple has had its share of controversies. The biggest one is the ongoing debate about whether XRP is a security, like stocks, or a currency, like the dollar. The U.S. Securities and Exchange Commission (SEC) is still deciding on this, and the outcome could have significant implications for Ripple. If they rule that XRP is a security, Ripple may face some hefty legal and financial consequences.

This is where the story gets a bit dicey. Ripple owns a lot of XRP, and they occasionally sell some to fund their operations. Critics argue that this is similar to a company issuing shares, which would make XRP more like a stock than a currency. Ripple, however, insists that XRP is a currency and should be treated as such.

While the debate rages on, Ripple has managed to make some pretty impressive partnerships. Big financial players like American Express and Santander have experimented with Ripple's technology. That's like the high school chess club getting endorsements from chess grandmasters—it's a big deal.

Investing in Ripple, like investing in any cryptocurrency, is a gamble. The price of XRP has been on a roller coaster ride—sometimes reaching impressive highs but also experiencing dramatic lows. If you're thinking of jumping on the Ripple bandwagon, remember that it's not for the faint-hearted. Prices can skyrocket, but they can plummet just as fast. And with the legal clouds hanging over it, the future of Ripple is as clear as mud.

But whether you're an investor or just a bystander, Ripple is undoubtedly a fascinating character in the grand saga of cryptocurrencies. It has a specific focus—making international money transfers faster and cheaper—which could genuinely improve lives. At the same time, it's surrounded by questions and controversies that add an element of drama to its story.

So, as you venture further into the world of cryptocurrencies, Ripple offers both a cautionary tale and a glimpse of a future where sending money is as easy as sending an email. Like any technological advance, it promises a lot but also comes with its own set of challenges and uncertainties. It's an unfolding story, and only time will tell if Ripple will succeed in its mission or end up as a footnote in the annals of digital currency history.

Litecoin

In the world of cryptocurrency, if Bitcoin is the golden child everyone talks about at family gatherings, then Litecoin is like its younger sibling—often overlooked but with its own unique qualities worth discussing. Created by a guy named Charlie Lee in 2011, Litecoin was designed to solve some of Bitcoin's problems and limitations.

Imagine you're in a race, and you're wearing heavy boots. Sure, those boots might protect you, but they slow you down. In a way, Bitcoin is like that—it's secure, but sometimes a bit slow and cumbersome when it comes to processing transactions. Litecoin, on the other hand, is like racing in lightweight sneakers. It was built to be faster and more efficient.

At the core, both Bitcoin and Litecoin function similarly. They're both decentralized digital currencies that operate on a technology called blockchain. Think of blockchain as a public ledger that records every transaction made. It's like a never-ending chain of digital "blocks" that are connected and secured.

So what makes Litecoin different? For starters, it processes transactions more quickly. Imagine you're in a checkout line at a grocery store. With Bitcoin, you might have to wait 10 minutes for the transaction to be confirmed. But with Litecoin, it takes just about 2.5 minutes. That's quicker than it takes to microwave your favorite popcorn!

But speed isn't Litecoin's only advantage. It also uses a different algorithm for mining. In simple terms, mining is how new coins are created and how transactions are added to the blockchain. Litecoin's algorithm is designed to be less demanding, which means that more people can participate in mining without needing expensive, specialized hardware.

Sounds great, right? Well, let's not get too ahead of ourselves. Litecoin has its share of challenges. One of the biggest is adoption. In the big crypto race, Bitcoin is way ahead when it comes to being accepted and used by businesses and individuals. It's like that popular kid in school who everyone wants to hang out with, while Litecoin is still trying to find its clique.

Another issue is its similarity to Bitcoin. Because Litecoin was created as an alternative to Bitcoin, rather than a complete reinvention, some people question its long-term value. It's a bit like having two types of soda that taste almost the same. Sure, some people might prefer one over the other, but many will question the need for both.

There's also the ever-present risk of volatility. If you think riding a roller coaster with loop-the-loops and sudden drops sounds thrilling yet scary, welcome to the world of cryptocurrency investing. The value of Litecoin, like all cryptocurrencies, can swing wildly from one day to the next. Investing in it is not for the faint of heart.

But despite these challenges, Litecoin has shown resilience. It has a strong community of supporters and developers who continue to improve its technology. It may not have reached the superstar status of Bitcoin, but it's consistently ranked among the top cryptocurrencies.

The story of Litecoin serves as a reminder that while Bitcoin might get most of the limelight, it's not the only cryptocurrency worth paying attention to. Whether you see Litecoin as a worthy competitor to Bitcoin or as a complement that fills in some of the gaps, it's an intriguing part of the cryptocurrency landscape.

Will Litecoin ever overtake Bitcoin? Will it carve out its own unique space and value? Or will it be overshadowed by newer, shinier options that come along? Only time will tell. But for now, Litecoin remains a key player in the world of digital currency, offering a slightly different take on what a cryptocurrency can be.

Just like in any family, every sibling has their own strengths and weaknesses, their own contributions to the bigger picture. Litecoin may be the younger sibling in the cryptocurrency family, but it has its own tale to tell—a tale of ambition, innovation, and the ongoing quest to make digital money faster, more efficient, and accessible to all. It's a story still in the making, and one worth keeping an eye on as the world of cryptocurrency continues to evolve.

And Others

By now, you've probably realized that the world of cryptocurrencies isn't a one-horse—or even a three-horse—race. Imagine walking into an ice cream shop and finding not just vanilla, chocolate, and strawberry, but a whole array of unique and exotic flavors. Some might cater to particular tastes, while others might have a specific use. That's exactly how the realm of cryptocurrencies works. Beyond Bitcoin, Ethereum, Ripple, and Litecoin, there are many other contenders in the field, each with its own unique selling points and challenges.

Take Cardano, for example. This cryptocurrency aims to provide a more secure and scalable blockchain and is known for its research-driven approach. Its founder, Charles Hoskinson, is also one of the co-founders of Ethereum. But what sets Cardano apart is its commitment to peer-reviewed scientific research as its backbone. The idea is to create a more secure and scalable blockchain, one that can handle more transactions and operate more efficiently. Think of it as building a car from scratch but only after consulting the best engineers, designers, and safety experts in the world.

Then there's Polkadot, another interesting player in the crypto arena. Its unique angle is "interoperability," which is just a fancy word for saying it aims to enable different blockchains to transfer messages and value in a trust-free fashion. Imagine a world where your iPhone could easily communicate with a friend's Android, sharing data seamlessly. That's what Polkadot is striving for in the world of blockchain.

But wait, there's more. Ever heard of Dogecoin? Initially started as a joke based on a popular internet meme featuring a Shiba Inu dog, Dogecoin has gained a surprising amount of traction and a devoted following. While it may not have the cutting-edge technological advancements of some other cryptocurrencies, it has captured the public's imagination. And in the world of finance and technology, sometimes that's more than enough to make an impact.

However, not all cryptocurrencies have a rosy path ahead of them. Like any new field, there are plenty of challenges. Regulation is a big one. Governments around the world are still grappling with how to deal with cryptocurrencies, and some have even banned them altogether. Then there's the issue of adoption. A cryptocurrency could have the most amazing features, but if businesses and consumers aren't using it, it's like a tree falling in an empty forest—no impact.

There's also the matter of competition. With new cryptocurrencies being launched all the time, standing out from the crowd becomes increasingly difficult. It's like auditioning for a role in a big movie, but the casting room is filled with hundreds of other talented actors. Each cryptocurrency needs a unique selling point, something that makes it different from the rest, just like each actor needs a way to catch the director's eye.

And of course, there's the risk factor. Investing in lesser-known cryptocurrencies can be like treasure hunting. You might find a hidden gem, or you might end up with fool's gold. Because the market is still young and volatile, prices can soar, but they can also plummet, leaving investors in a lurch.

In the grand tapestry of the cryptocurrency world, these "other" coins—often referred to as 'altcoins'—each add their own unique color and texture. They may not always make headlines like Bitcoin or Ethereum, but they are a crucial part of the ecosystem, pushing the boundaries of what's possible and challenging the status quo.

The tale of these other cryptocurrencies is like an anthology of short stories, each contributing to the larger narrative of this financial revolution. They serve as a reminder that innovation is often a collective endeavor, with each player bringing something different to the table. While the journey of each may be filled with ups and downs, triumphs and setbacks, their presence enriches the broader story of what digital money can be.

Whether any of these other cryptocurrencies will rise to the level of Bitcoin or Ethereum is a question for the future. For now, they offer a fascinating glimpse into the diversity and dynamism that characterize this ever-evolving landscape. It's a narrative still being written, and each of these 'other' cryptocurrencies has a chapter in it. What that chapter says is up to them—and to us.

5.3 ICOs and Tokens

If cryptocurrencies like Bitcoin and Ethereum are the pioneers settling new lands in the world of digital money, then Initial Coin Offerings, or ICOs, are the fundraising campaigns to support those expeditions. Just like a company might offer shares of its stock to raise money for new projects or expansion, in the crypto world, businesses or developers often offer tokens. It's an entirely new way of drumming up support and funding, a bit like a digital version of the California Gold Rush. But as with any quest for treasure, there are both rewards and pitfalls, booms and busts.

Now, what's a token, you ask? A token is a special type of cryptocurrency that's not quite a standalone currency like Bitcoin. Instead, it's usually tied to a specific project or company. Imagine if, instead of buying a ticket to a movie, you bought a "MovieCoin" that could only be used at specific theaters for specific films. That's sort of what a token is like—specialized money for a specialized purpose.

But here's where things get intriguing. In the world of crypto, these tokens can also represent other kinds of assets. They can be like digital deeds to virtual land in an online game, or they can represent a share in a real-world piece of art. The possibilities are just beginning to be explored. It's like we're explorers, standing at the edge of an undiscovered continent, with a whole new world of opportunities and challenges stretching out in front of us.

Because ICOs and tokens are a relatively new phenomenon, they've become a bit of a Wild West. There's potential for great fortune, but there are also plenty of risks. Fraud and scams have been a problem, like snake oil salesmen of the past, luring in unsuspecting folks with promises of quick riches. Regulation is still catching up, and many people have lost money investing in ICOs that turned out to be less than legitimate. Imagine diving into a treasure chest, only to find out it's filled with fool's gold. That's a risk you run in this untamed landscape.

At the same time, ICOs have revolutionized the way projects and companies can get funding. Traditional ways of raising money often involve lots of middlemen—banks, lawyers, and regulatory bodies, just to name a few. With an ICO, a startup can go directly to the public, offering their tokens in exchange for established cryptocurrencies like Bitcoin or Ethereum. It's like a public audition where you get to choose the next big star—except, in this case, you're choosing which projects deserve to get off the ground. And if those projects succeed, the value of your tokens could skyrocket, turning a small initial investment into a considerable sum.

The ICO model has been especially popular among tech startups. But its influence is spreading to other sectors as well, from real estate to entertainment to supply chain management. Like a viral video that starts off with a few views but quickly spreads, the impact of ICOs and tokens is rippling across various industries, challenging traditional models of fundraising and investment.

So, as you learn more about ICOs and tokens along your journey, remember that you're navigating through a world that's still defining its rules, a world that's filled with both immense promise and considerable risk. It's like being a settler in a new land. You're not sure what challenges you'll face or what opportunities you'll find, but you know it's an adventure worth embarking on. And like any good adventure, it's not just the destination that counts; it's also how you get there and what you learn along the way.

5.4 The Rise of NFTs

Non-Fungible Tokens, or NFTs for short, are like the rare, limited edition baseball cards of the digital world. Only, instead of a baseball card that you can hold in your hand, an NFT is a unique piece of digital property, whether it's artwork, music, or even a tweet. Yep, you heard that right. People are spending real money to own things that exist only on the internet.

You may wonder, "Why on Earth would anyone pay for something they can just look at online for free?" Well, it's all about ownership and uniqueness. Just like owning an original painting by a famous artist, owning an NFT means you possess something that no one else has in the exact same way. It's verified, it's unique, and it's yours.

But wait, isn't the internet all about sharing and copying? How can something be 'unique' online when you can just screenshot it? Here's where it gets interesting. NFTs exist on something called the blockchain, a kind of digital ledger that's decentralized and impossible to tamper with. When you own an NFT, the blockchain records that ownership, proving beyond a doubt that you're the legitimate owner. It's like having a notary public for the internet, stamping their seal of approval on your digital asset.

Just like original works of art, NFTs have been selling for incredible amounts of money. We're talking millions of dollars for a single piece. But why? The answer lies in value and rarity. When something is rare, people often see it as valuable. Remember those baseball cards? Some of them are worth a fortune today because they're scarce. Similarly, the idea that a particular digital item can be 'rare' is intriguing to many. And like any rare commodity, people are willing to pay top dollar for it.

However, it's not all sunshine and rainbows in the world of NFTs. Like any burgeoning industry, it has its fair share of problems. For starters, there are questions about copyright and intellectual property. If someone takes a screenshot of your tweet and turns it into an NFT, who owns that? The blockchain might say one thing, but the law might say another.

Another issue is the environmental impact. You see, the same blockchain technology that makes NFTs possible also uses a ton of energy. It's a bit like having a car that can do amazing things but burns a ton of gas doing it. Many are concerned about how sustainable this is in the long run, especially as the world grapples with climate change.

Also, because NFTs are so new, they're not very well regulated. That opens the door to scams and fraud. Just as there were counterfeiters in the days of the Gold Rush, there are digital counterfeiters today. They'll create fake NFTs or trick people into buying something that's not as valuable as it seems. Always remember, not everything that glitters is gold.

But even with these problems, the rise of NFTs is undeniably shaping the future of how we think about ownership and value in the digital age. For artists and creators, it's an entirely new way to monetize their work. Instead of making money from prints or merchandising, they can sell NFTs of their digital art. And for collectors, it's a whole new frontier of items to acquire and invest in.

As we forge ahead into this relatively unknown territory, the importance of understanding the complexities and nuances can't be overstated. NFTs are neither a magical solution to all problems nor a passing fad that'll be forgotten tomorrow. They represent a seismic shift in our perception of value, ownership, and the concept of rarity, translated into the digital domain. And like any seismic shift, it brings both opportunities and challenges.

So, when it comes to NFTs, the best advice is the same as it would be for any journey into uncharted territory: proceed with caution, but also with curiosity. Keep your eyes open, your wits about you, and be prepared for surprises around every corner. As we pull back the curtain on this new, exciting chapter in the digital revolution, who knows what we'll find? It's like being a treasure hunter in a digital world, and this, dear reader, is our map.

5.5 Key Takeaways

1. Non-Fungible Tokens (NFTs) are unique digital assets verified on a blockchain. They're like rare collectibles, only digital.
2.
3. The allure of NFTs lies in their uniqueness and the blockchain's ability to prove who the true owner is, adding a layer of value and scarcity.
4. NFTs have sold for incredible amounts of money, largely because people see value in owning something rare and unique.
5. There are pressing concerns around NFTs, such as copyright issues, environmental impact due to energy-intensive blockchain technology, and the potential for scams.
6. NFTs are redefining how we think about ownership and value in the digital world, offering new opportunities and challenges for artists, collectors, and investors alike.
7. As the NFT landscape evolves, it's crucial to approach it with both caution and curiosity, understanding that this is a complex and ever-changing space.

Part III: Understanding Blockchain Technology

Section 6: Blockchain: The Technology Behind Cryptocurrency

You've probably heard the term "blockchain" thrown around in conversations about Bitcoin and other cryptocurrencies. But what does it really mean? At its core, blockchain is a digital ledger. Imagine a massive notebook where every transaction ever made is recorded, except that this notebook isn't stored in one place. Instead, copies of it are kept on computers all around the world.

Now, you might be wondering why we need a separate chapter just to talk about a digital notebook. Ah, but this isn't just any notebook. This notebook has a couple of neat tricks up its sleeve.

First off, once something is written into this notebook, it can't be easily altered or removed. Let's say you and a friend decide to trade baseball cards. You give your friend your Babe Ruth card in exchange for their Jackie Robinson card. Once you've made the trade, you can't go back and claim that you never gave away your Babe Ruth card. The blockchain, like a super-reliable witness, makes sure of that.

Second, this ledger is decentralized, meaning no single person or entity controls it. Imagine if everyone in your school had an exact copy of your report card, and if an error was made, it would have to be corrected on every single copy. That would make it pretty hard for anyone to change your grades without everyone else knowing, wouldn't it?

So why does any of this matter? Well, blockchain technology is what makes cryptocurrencies like Bitcoin work. Without blockchain, Bitcoin would be like a car without an engine. This underlying technology ensures that all transactions are transparent, secure, and—most importantly—can't be tampered with.

And it's not just about money. Believe it or not, blockchain has the potential to change the way we do a lot of things, not just how we handle our finances. From healthcare to voting systems, this technology could revolutionize a lot of industries. Imagine being able to vote from the comfort of your home without worrying about voter fraud. Or think about a hospital instantly having access to your medical records without the need for a pile of paperwork. Sounds pretty cool, right?

However, blockchain technology isn't without its flaws. For starters, the same thing that makes it secure—its decentralized nature—also makes it slow. And we're not talking turtle slow; we're talking snail slow. Why? Because updating the blockchain requires a consensus from all its users, which takes time. And then there's the energy consumption. You know how we're all supposed to be doing our part to help the environment? Well, blockchain networks, particularly ones that use a method called "proof of work," consume a lot of energy, which isn't exactly helping Mother Earth.

Another issue to consider is the steep learning curve. Blockchain technology is complex and can be hard to understand. That's why you're here, reading this book. We're going to break down the ins and outs of blockchain technology, so you can understand how it works and why it's so important.

In the chapters that follow, we're going to dive into the nuts and bolts of blockchain. We'll explore how it was developed, the problems it solves, and the challenges it faces. So buckle up, because this is going to be a thrilling ride through the digital frontier.

And remember, just like any frontier, there are both opportunities and pitfalls. As we wade into the waters of blockchain technology, it's crucial to keep both in mind. Are you ready? Let's dive in.

6.1 The Basics of a Blockchain

So, let's talk about this digital notebook, also known as a blockchain. It's like the heartbeat of cryptocurrencies. Without it, the whole system falls apart. But before we dive into all the technical stuff, let's take a step back. You've probably played the game "telephone" before, right? One person whispers a message into another person's ear, and it goes down the line until the last person says it out loud. The fun part? The message usually gets mixed up along the way.

Now, imagine if you had a notebook where the original message was written down, and as it got passed down the line, each person had to agree that the message matched what was written. There would be fewer mix-ups, right? That's one way to think about how a blockchain works. It keeps track of information in a way that's hard to mess up.

Okay, enough analogies. Let's get into the meat and potatoes.

First off, what's in this digital notebook? Well, each page of this notebook is what we call a "block." And what's written on these blocks are "transactions." If I pay you 10 Bitcoins for a rare comic book, that transaction goes into a block. Simple enough? But wait, there's more.

Each block also has something called a "hash." Think of a hash as a unique fingerprint for that block. No two blocks can have the same hash. So, each block is unique, like a snowflake. But what makes blockchain super special is that each block also contains the hash of the previous block. That's why it's called a "chain" of blocks. Each block is linked to the one before it. If you tried to mess with one block, you'd have to mess with all the blocks that come after it. And that's no easy feat.

So, you've got this chain of blocks, all connected like a digital train. The question is, who's driving this train? The answer: nobody and everybody. Remember, this is a decentralized system. That means there's no single person, company, or government running the show. Instead, it's a network of computers, known as "nodes," that all have copies of the blockchain. When a new transaction happens, all the nodes get updated. It's like a group project where everyone has to agree before anything gets done.

But how do these nodes agree on what goes into a new block? That's where "mining" comes in. In the world of blockchain, mining isn't about pickaxes and gold nuggets. It's about solving complex math problems. These problems are so hard that they require powerful computers to solve them. And the first computer to solve it gets to add the new block to the chain. As a reward, the miner usually gets some of the cryptocurrency.

Now, you might be thinking, "Wait a minute. If anyone can add a block, what's stopping someone from adding a fake transaction?" Great question. The answer is the blockchain itself. Because each block is connected to the one before it, changing one block would require changing all the subsequent blocks as well. And remember, you'd need the agreement of all the nodes in the network. It's like trying to cheat on a test when the entire class is watching you. Good luck with that.

But the system isn't perfect. One issue is the sheer amount of computer power needed for mining. These computers need a lot of electricity to run, which isn't great for our planet. Plus, because the math problems are so hard, it takes a while to add a new block. That's why transactions can sometimes be slow. It's the price we pay for security and transparency.

Another challenge is what's known as a "51% attack." If someone controls more than half of the network's computing power, they could theoretically add fraudulent transactions. But pulling off such an attack would be incredibly difficult and expensive. It's like trying to rig a school election when everyone's keeping an eye on the ballot box. Not so easy, is it?

So there you have it: the basics of a blockchain. It's a digital notebook that keeps track of transactions, made up of individual blocks, each with its own unique hash. It's decentralized, meaning no single entity is in charge. And it uses complex math problems to keep everything secure.

It's easy to get lost in the buzzwords and technical jargon, but at its core, blockchain is a revolution in how we handle information. It's about creating a system where trust is built in, not bolted on. And while it's not without its problems, its potential to change the way we live and work is pretty astounding. So, as we move forward, keep in mind that understanding blockchain is like holding the key to a whole new world. Are you ready to unlock it?

6.2 How Blocks and Chains Work

So, we've talked about the "what" of blockchain, but let's dive a bit deeper into the "how." The term "blockchain" itself gives away some clues. It's a chain made of blocks, right? But it's not just any chain, and certainly not just any blocks. This chain is a super-secure digital ledger that keeps everyone honest. But how do these blocks and chains actually work? Well, let's break it down.

First, let's talk about the block itself. Imagine a wooden block, and on each side, you can write some information. In a blockchain block, you can store things like transactions—say, Bob sent Alice 5 Bitcoins—or maybe even a contract. And just like how a wooden block has unique grains and patterns, each blockchain block has a unique identifier known as a "hash." This hash makes sure that each block is different from every other block.

But a block doesn't stand alone. It's part of a community—part of a chain. Imagine you're building a tower with your blocks. Each block sits on top of another, and to keep them secure, you might glue them together. Well, the "hash" is like that glue, but even stronger. Each block in a blockchain contains its own hash and the hash of the block that came before it. So, if someone tries to mess with one block, the rest of the chain can say, "Hey, something's not right here," and the change won't be accepted.

This is one of the coolest parts about blockchain: its security. Imagine trying to rob a bank, but the bank is spread out in pieces all over the city. If you tried to break into one part, alarms in all the other parts would start ringing like crazy. That's what it's like trying to hack a blockchain. Change one block, and you'd have to change every block that comes after it—and you'd have to do this faster than the network can add new blocks. And trust me, that's next to impossible.

So who gets to add new blocks? Ah, that's a great question. In blockchain land, we have people called "miners." But they're not the kind who wear hard hats and carry pickaxes. These miners use computers—powerful ones—to solve really tough math problems. Imagine you have a lock, and the key is a super-complicated math equation. The miner's job is to figure out the solution that unlocks it. The first one to do it gets to add the new block to the chain.

And what do miners get for all this hard work? Well, they usually get some cryptocurrency, like Bitcoin. It's like a reward for being good at math and having a fast computer. But remember, because the math problems are really hard, mining uses a lot of energy. That's something a lot of people are worried about when it comes to blockchain's impact on the planet.

You might wonder, "If it's so secure, why do we need miners to keep solving these problems?" The answer is a bit like asking why we need locks on our doors if we live in a safe neighborhood. The problems add an extra layer of security. They make sure that no one can just waltz in and add a block. The work the miners do validates and secures every transaction.

But it's not all perfect. For instance, there's something known as a "51% attack." This is when one group of miners controls more than half of the network's computing power. If this happens, they could, in theory, approve fraudulent transactions. It's a bit like if one team had all the best players in a sports game; the balance would be tipped unfairly. However, pulling this off would be extremely hard and costly, and the more people use and secure a blockchain, the less likely this becomes.

Another downside? Speed. Because every transaction needs to be verified by this network of computers, things can sometimes slow down. It's like waiting in line at a grocery store that only has one checkout lane open. Everyone has to wait their turn, which can take time.

So, let's recap: A block is like a page in a digital notebook, where transactions are recorded. When it's filled, it's sealed with a unique fingerprint—a hash—and joins a chain of previous blocks. Miners, using intense computing power, validate these blocks by solving complex math problems. This all adds up to a super-secure system that's tough to cheat, although it does have a few challenges to overcome.

We've talked a lot about blocks, chains, miners, and math. But what's incredible is how this technology, despite its complexities and flaws, is paving the way for a future where trust is built into the system, not just added on as an afterthought. It's more than a technological marvel; it's a new way of thinking about how we interact, trade, and trust each other in the digital age.

So as we keep going, remember: each block, each chain, and each miner plays a role in this intricate dance. And you, by understanding it, are part of this exciting frontier too. Ready to explore more? Let's go.

6.3 Importance of Blockchain in Cryptocurrency

Alright, so we've gone through the nuts and bolts of how blocks and chains work. But why is all of this so critical when we're talking about cryptocurrency? After all, couldn't we just use regular databases and computer systems to keep track of who owns what? Well, we could, but that would be like choosing to paddle a canoe when you have a speedboat available. Blockchain technology brings a whole new level of game-changing features to the world of money, especially cryptocurrency.

Let's start with trust. In the traditional way of doing things, you trust a bank to hold onto your money, and you trust a credit card company to handle your transactions. It works, but sometimes, things go wrong. Banks can make mistakes. Credit card companies can get hacked. You're putting your trust in a handful of people you've never met. Blockchain changes that by spreading the trust around, kind of like sprinkling magic trust dust over an entire network of computers. It's no longer one institution you have to trust; it's a system that keeps itself honest.

And how does it do that? We talked about miners and how they secure transactions. Well, that's part of it. The decentralized network—fancy words to say it's spread out over lots of computers—also plays a huge role in maintaining trust. Imagine a classroom where every student is also the teacher. If one student tries to cheat on a test, the others will catch him or her immediately. The same concept applies here: everyone in the network has access to the blockchain, so if something's off, it'll be noticed.

Let's talk about speed and cost. In the world we live in, sending money across the globe can be slow and expensive. There's currency exchange, bank fees, and delays. But in the realm of blockchain and cryptocurrency, that all changes. It's like a highway with no speed limit and no toll booths. You can send Bitcoin from America to Australia as easily as emailing a friend who lives down the street. And usually, it's way cheaper. Why? Because you're cutting out the middlemen—those banks and service providers who take a slice of your money for themselves.

You might be thinking, "If it's so great, why isn't everyone using it?" Good question. One reason is that it's still new. Imagine being one of the first people to use the internet or a cellphone. It takes time for people to understand it, trust it, and integrate it into their lives. And let's be honest, not everyone's comfortable with such big changes, especially when it comes to money.

Then there are regulatory and legal issues. Laws are like rules for a giant societal game, but the game board keeps changing with technologies like blockchain. Governments are scratching their heads, trying to figure out how to regulate this new kind of money and the technology behind it. It's like creating new rules for a sport that's still being invented.

Moreover, blockchain technology isn't just about money. It's bigger than that. Think about voting. We all know voting is critical for a democracy, but it's not always easy to trust that every vote was counted or that the system is secure. Enter blockchain. With its level of security and transparency, it could revolutionize the way we vote, making it easier to vote and harder to cheat.

And what about contracts? These days, making a contract means filling out a bunch of paperwork, getting lawyers involved, and jumping through legal hoops. With blockchain, you can create "smart contracts" that execute themselves when certain conditions are met. Imagine setting up a lemonade stand where the pitcher automatically refills itself whenever it's empty. That's the kind of efficiency we're talking about.

Now, as incredible as blockchain is, it's not without challenges. We've talked about how it consumes a lot of energy. Then there are issues of scalability. The more people use a blockchain, the bigger it gets, and the more power it needs. Engineers are hustling to solve these problems, but they're like puzzle pieces that haven't all been fitted together yet.

So let's take a step back and soak this in. Blockchain technology is more than just a fad or a buzzword; it's a groundbreaking way to think about trust, money, and information. Whether it's securing your Bitcoin, making sure your vote counts, or simplifying contracts, blockchain is shaking up the way we do things. And like any great story, it's filled with twists, challenges, and a dash of mystery.

Remember, you're not just reading about this technology; you're living in the time when it's all unfolding. One day you might look back and tell stories about how you were there when the world started trusting in blocks and chains, instead of banks and bureaucrats.

And so, the blockchain continues to grow, one block at a time, and we're all a part of this intricate, fascinating chain of human endeavor and digital innovation. This isn't just tech talk; this is a shift in how society operates, and it's happening right now. Ready to dig deeper? Let's keep going.

6.4 Decentralization

Alright, let's dive into a word you've probably heard buzzing around a lot when people talk about blockchain and cryptocurrency: decentralization. Sounds fancy, right? But what does it actually mean, and why is it a big deal?

Imagine a spider web. In the middle, you have the spider, who's in charge of everything. He's the one who fixes the web when it breaks and catches the food. That's what we call a "centralized" system. Just like how a bank is in charge of keeping your money safe, the spider is in charge of the whole web. But what happens if something happens to the spider? The whole web falls apart.

Now, imagine a different kind of web. Instead of one spider in the middle, you have lots of smaller spiders, each taking care of their own part of the web. That's "decentralization," and it's the cornerstone of blockchain technology.

In a decentralized network, like a blockchain, there's no single point of control. It's like a team sport where every player is also the referee. The responsibility is spread out, so no single player—or computer, in our case—has too much power or control. This makes it harder for any single point to fail or for any one person to cheat the system. Think about it, if you're playing a game and everyone is watching, you're less likely to cheat, right?

That might sound good, but it also brings some challenges. In a classroom, if you have one teacher, it's easy to know who's in charge and what the rules are. But if every student is also a teacher, things might get a bit chaotic. Who decides what the homework is? Who makes sure everyone's playing fair? That's where blockchain's rules and algorithms come into play. They act like the rulebook that everyone has to follow, ensuring that all the transactions are valid and everything runs smoothly.

So, why is this idea of decentralization so revolutionary?

First off, it's all about security. In a centralized system, if someone hacks into the main computer, they could mess up everything. But in a decentralized system, like a blockchain, they'd have to hack into the majority of computers on the network to pull off anything sneaky. That's like trying to rob a neighborhood where every single house has its own high-tech security system.

Another thing is transparency. In a centralized system, you have to trust that the main computer (or the people running it) is keeping accurate records. It's a bit like playing a game where only one person can see the scoreboard. But in a decentralized system, the scoreboard is visible to everyone. You don't have to trust a single entity; you can verify everything yourself.

But wait, there's more. Decentralization also opens up the doors to innovation and competition. In a centralized system, the main hub controls what happens. They set the rules of the game, and if you want to play, you have to follow their rules. But in a decentralized world, anyone can join and contribute. It's like a community garden where anyone can come and plant their seeds. This kind of open-access environment fosters creativity and speeds up progress. It's like being in a race where everyone's pushing each other to run faster and break new records.

However, it's not all sunshine and rainbows. Decentralization brings its own set of challenges. One issue is that it can be inefficient. In a centralized system, you have one main computer that can make quick decisions. But in a decentralized network, you need consensus, which means getting a majority of computers to agree. This can take time and a lot of computational power. It's the difference between one chef deciding what's for dinner and having to ask every single person in a big family what they want to eat.

Another challenge is the issue of responsibility. If something goes wrong in a centralized system, you know who's to blame: the central authority. But in a decentralized system, the lines of accountability can get blurry. If everyone's in charge, then who takes the fall when things go sideways?

So, is decentralization the future? It's hard to say. Right now, it's like a science experiment that we're all part of. Some people believe it will revolutionize everything from finance to voting to the internet itself. Others are more skeptical, wary of the challenges and risks.

What we do know is that decentralization is already changing the way we think about systems and authority. It's taking power from the few and giving it to the many, rewriting the rules of who gets to control information, money, and even the way we interact with each other.

And like any great story, this one's still being written. It has heroes and villains, challenges and triumphs. And you, whether you're simply using a cryptocurrency wallet or diving into the nuts and bolts of blockchain, are a part of it. So, buckle up, because it's going to be an interesting ride. Let's see where this road of blocks and chains takes us.

6.5 Public vs Private Blockchains

We've talked a lot about blockchains, those digital ledgers that keep track of transactions, but did you know not all blockchains are the same? That's right. Blockchains come in different flavors, kind of like ice cream. And just like you might prefer vanilla to chocolate, different organizations and people have different needs when it comes to blockchains. So let's get into it: what's the difference between a public and a private blockchain?

Imagine your school's playground. Any kid can join in a game of soccer or hopscotch. It's open for all. That's like a public blockchain. Anyone can join, participate, and look at the transactions happening on it. It's what we call "permissionless," meaning you don't need special permission to join in.

Now picture a private clubhouse, maybe a treehouse in someone's backyard. To get in, you need to know the secret handshake or password. That's similar to a private blockchain. You can't just join; you need an invitation or approval from the people in charge. They decide who gets to see the transactions and who gets to participate. It's "permissioned," the opposite of permissionless.

So what are some of the pros and cons of each?

Public Blockchains

Let's start with public blockchains. The big draw here is that they're, well, public. Anyone can join, which means they're more decentralized. If you remember from our last chapter, decentralization is a bit like having multiple spiders take care of a web instead of just one. It adds layers of security and transparency. Since everyone can see the transactions, it's harder to cheat or hide anything sneaky.

Public blockchains are also more open to innovation. Remember the community garden example? Anyone can come in and plant a seed, so you end up with a vibrant mix of flowers and vegetables. Similarly, public blockchains can grow and evolve quickly because they're open to everyone's input.

But it's not all roses. Public blockchains can be slower and more costly to operate. Think about that game of soccer on the playground. If anyone can join, it might get crowded and chaotic. The more players there are, the harder it is to score a goal. Public blockchains face the same issue. The more people participate, the harder it is to reach a consensus or agreement on transactions. This can slow things down and use up a lot of computing power, which isn't very efficient or eco-friendly.

Private Blockchains

Now, what about private blockchains? The biggest advantage here is control. In a private blockchain, the rules of the game are set by the people who started it. This can make things more efficient. Imagine playing soccer with just your friends instead of the whole school. It's easier to keep track of the ball, and the game moves more quickly.

Private blockchains are also more secure in some ways. Because not everyone can join, there's less chance of someone coming in just to mess things up. It's like having a security guard at the door of that private clubhouse.

However, private blockchains have their downsides too. For one, they're not as transparent. If the people in charge want to change the rules or hide certain transactions, they can. It's a bit like playing a game where only one team knows the score. Plus, because they're more centralized, they're vulnerable to the same kinds of problems we talked about with centralization—like what happens if the main computer or authority figure is compromised?

The Middle Ground: Consortium Blockchains

There's also a middle ground known as consortium blockchains. These are semi-private, kind of like a VIP section in a public event. A group of organizations manages it, rather than a single one. This allows for a bit of both worlds. They're less open than public blockchains but offer more transparency than a fully private one.

The Verdict

So, which is better: public or private blockchains? Well, that's like asking if chocolate ice cream is better than vanilla. It really depends on what you're looking for.

Public blockchains offer more transparency and freedom, but they can be slower and less efficient. Private blockchains give you more control and efficiency, but you sacrifice some transparency and openness.

In the end, the "best" type of blockchain depends on what you need it for. Are you building a community project where anyone should be allowed to contribute? A public blockchain might be the way to go. Are you a business looking to streamline its operations with more control over who sees what? Then a private blockchain could be a better fit.

It's like choosing the right tool for the job. And just like any tool, blockchains—whether public or private—have their strengths and weaknesses. Knowing what those are is the first step in figuring out which one is right for you.

So there you have it, a journey through the landscape of public and private blockchains, each with its own set of opportunities and challenges. As you dig deeper into the world of cryptocurrency and blockchain technology, understanding this distinction will be like having a map on a complex hike. You'll know better which paths to explore and which ones to perhaps avoid.

In this unfolding story of blockchain, the choice between public and private is a pivotal one, shaping not just the chapters to come but also influencing the writers—like you—who are helping to pen this transformative tale.

6.6 Key Takeaways

We've just navigated some winding trails through the world of blockchain technology, uncovering not just its structure but also its soul. The mechanisms that make it tick are deeply entangled with the values it stands for. Before we step further into this jungle of innovation, let's pause and reflect on the key points we've covered:

1. **Different Flavors:** Blockchains aren't one-size-fits-all. They come in different types: public, private, and consortium. Knowing the differences between them is like having a roadmap for your journey into the world of cryptocurrency.
2. **Public Blockchains:** These are open to anyone. They're "permissionless," which means you don't need an invite to join. Public blockchains are known for their transparency and openness but can be slower and less efficient.
3. **Private Blockchains:** Unlike their public cousins, private blockchains are "permissioned." They're not open to everyone, offering more control and efficiency at the expense of reduced transparency.
4. **Consortium Blockchains:** A happy medium between public and private, these are managed by a group of organizations. They're like the VIP section in a public event, allowing for more control without completely shutting out transparency.
5. **Pros and Cons:** Both public and private blockchains have their strengths and weaknesses. Public ones are transparent but can be less efficient. Private ones are more controlled but risk a lack of transparency.
6. **Decentralization:** One of the core advantages of public blockchains is decentralization, which adds layers of security and transparency. Private blockchains, because of their closed nature, are generally more centralized.
7. **Efficiency vs. Openness:** Public blockchains allow for more innovation but can be bogged down by their open nature.

Private blockchains are generally quicker and more efficient but limit who can participate, which can stifle innovation.
8. **Tailored Needs:** The best blockchain for you or your organization depends on your specific needs. It's all about choosing the right tool for the job.
9. **Influence and Control:** The type of blockchain also affects how much influence participants have. In public blockchains, changes are often community-driven. In private ones, a single entity usually holds more sway.
10. **Pivotal Choices:** The blockchain you choose can significantly impact your experience in the cryptocurrency world. It's a choice that sets the stage for all the other decisions you'll make in this arena.

Understanding these takeaways is like having a compass in this adventurous world of blockchain technology. It won't tell you exactly where to go, but it will certainly help you make more informed decisions as you navigate through.

So, there you have it—the high notes on the soundtrack of this blockchain journey. As we gear up for the next part of our adventure, remember, each choice you make shapes the story. Choose wisely.

Section 7: Blockchain Use-Cases

Just like the internet isn't only for sending emails or searching for information, blockchain isn't just for Bitcoin or other cryptocurrencies. This groundbreaking technology has applications—use-cases, as people in the know like to call them—that reach far beyond the realm of digital money. In this section, we're going to dive deep into some of these fascinating applications that are changing the way various industries operate.

Remember when we talked about the blockchain being a kind of ledger, a record-keeping tool? Well, imagine that same ledger keeping track of not just transactions, but almost anything you can think of: contracts, medical records, even how fresh the food is in your local grocery store. If this sounds a bit like science fiction, I assure you, it's not. We're already living in a world where blockchain is beginning to reshape sectors from healthcare to supply chains, from art to real estate, and from energy to even the way we vote.

Healthcare: First off, let's talk about an industry that touches everyone's life—the healthcare sector. Medical records are confidential, sensitive, and extremely important. The way we handle them now is, let's just say, not as secure as it could be. But with blockchain technology, medical records could be stored in a way that's not only safe but also easy to share between different healthcare providers.

Supply Chains: If you've ever wondered where your food comes from, or how the materials for your phone or computer are sourced, blockchain has some answers for you. The technology can trace the entire journey of a product, from the factory or farm right to your doorstep. This has enormous potential to make supply chains more efficient and transparent.

Art and Intellectual Property: For artists and creators, proving ownership of their work is a big deal. Thanks to blockchain, there's now a more reliable way to prove who created a piece of art or music. This is great not only for artists but also for buyers who want to make sure they're getting the real deal.

Real Estate: Buying a house is one of the biggest decisions you'll ever make. It's also a process filled with paperwork, legal hurdles, and the constant worry that something might go wrong. Blockchain can simplify this process by securely and transparently handling the legal aspects of buying and selling property.

Energy Sector: Imagine a future where you could sell excess energy from your solar panels directly to your neighbors without going through the grid. Blockchain could make this possible, creating more efficient and sustainable energy systems.

Voting: Think about the last time you voted. Maybe you stood in a long line, or maybe you mailed in your ballot. However you did it, did you wonder if your vote was actually counted, or if the election was entirely fair? Blockchain technology could revolutionize the way we vote, making the process more secure and transparent than ever before.

Now, you might be thinking, "Wow, blockchain can do all that?" Yes, it's not just a one-trick pony. The technology has immense potential to revolutionize various aspects of our daily lives, often in ways we can't yet fully comprehend.

The real power of blockchain isn't just in creating cryptocurrencies; it's in providing solutions to problems we didn't even know could be solved. It's the Swiss Army knife of the digital age, a tool with a wide range of applications that can make our lives simpler, safer, and more efficient.

So, get ready for a whirlwind tour of the many different landscapes where blockchain is making waves. We'll explore each one, digging into the details and painting a picture of a future reshaped by this incredible technology.

Hold on to your seats. This journey through the world of blockchain use-cases is about to get really interesting.

7.1 Financial Services

Let's start where blockchain first made its mark—the world of money, or more precisely, the complex web we call financial services. From buying a candy bar to saving for college, everything you do with money flows through this system. Right now, that system works like a maze, full of twists, turns, and sometimes, dead ends. Banks, credit card companies, stock exchanges—they're all part of this financial puzzle, and frankly, they're not as efficient or as fair as they could be.

Here's a little scenario for you. Imagine you have an aunt who lives in another country, and she wants to send you some money for your birthday. In the current system, that money has to jump through multiple hoops, and each hoop takes a piece of the cake. By the time it reaches you, your birthday gift might be smaller than your aunt intended. Not to mention, it can take days, sometimes even weeks, for that money to find its way to your bank account. Frustrating, right?

Well, blockchain has the power to change all that.

Instant Transactions: In a blockchain system, your aunt's birthday gift to you could happen in the blink of an eye. We're talking seconds, maybe minutes, but definitely not days. Why? Because blockchain technology can make transactions almost instant, no matter where in the world you are.

Lower Fees: Remember those hoops that take a slice of your cake? They're usually charging fees for the service they provide, and those fees can add up. With blockchain, those middlemen might not be necessary, which means fewer fees for you and your aunt.

Security: This is a big one. Banks and other financial institutions hold a lot of your personal information. Your name, your address, and way more details about your life than you'd like to think about. That information is a gold mine for hackers, and it's not as safe as it should be. Blockchain technology can encrypt this information, making it extremely tough for anyone who shouldn't have access to get their hands on it.

Transparency: Ever wonder where your money actually goes when you invest it or put it in a savings account? With blockchain, you can track every transaction. That doesn't mean you'll have to become a detective to find out where your money is going, but if you wanted to, you could.

Stocks and Investments: Even the stock market could get a makeover from blockchain. Buying and selling stocks could become as straightforward as sending an email. And because everything is transparent, the chances of foul play, like fraud, could be reduced.

Smart Contracts: Now, let's get a bit futuristic. Imagine you're buying a car. Normally, this involves a bunch of paperwork and maybe a notary to make sure everyone's keeping their promises. In a blockchain world, a "smart contract" could handle all of that automatically. The moment you pay the agreed price, the car's digital ownership would switch over to you, no paperwork needed.

So, how does blockchain pull off these financial magic tricks? It uses complex algorithms and a decentralized network of computers to verify transactions. Once verified, these transactions are added to a chain of records that anyone can see but no one can alter. This is what makes the system quick, secure, and transparent.

Now, this doesn't mean that banks and financial institutions are going to vanish into thin air. They still have roles to play, but blockchain could force them to evolve, to become better versions of themselves.

What we're looking at here is a financial revolution. A change in how we handle money, making it faster, safer, and more democratic. And remember, we're just scratching the surface. The possibilities are almost endless, and the story of blockchain in financial services is still being written.

So, as you think about your own money—whether it's your weekly allowance, your first paycheck, or your college fund—remember that the world of financial services could be very different by the time you're making big financial choices. And much of that change could come thanks to blockchain.

7.2 Supply Chain Management

Let's shift gears for a moment. Instead of talking about money, let's talk about stuff. You know, the everyday things you use: your phone, your shoes, even the food you eat. Ever wonder how these things get to you? They don't just magically appear on store shelves or at your doorstep. Each product has a journey, and that journey is what we call a supply chain.

A supply chain is like a relay race. Imagine a team of runners passing a baton from one to another until they reach the finish line. Each runner has a specific job, whether it's to start the race strong or to sprint the final leg. Similarly, a product goes through multiple steps— from manufacturing to shipping to finally landing in your hands.

Sounds straightforward, right? Not so fast. The supply chain can be complicated, slow, and filled with errors. Sometimes, products get lost. Sometimes, they get damaged. And sometimes, you just don't know where they came from. That's a big deal when we're talking about things like food safety or ethical manufacturing.

Enter blockchain, the technology that promises to streamline this complex process.

Tracking Products: Imagine scanning a QR code on a bag of apples and instantly knowing where those apples were grown, when they were picked, and how they got to the store. Blockchain can store all that information, making it easier for you to make informed choices.

Faster Shipments: Right now, shipping products can involve a lot of red tape. There are forms to fill out, inspections to pass, and often, delays that nobody can explain. Blockchain can speed up this process by automating many of these steps.

Reducing Errors: Remember that relay race? If one runner drops the baton, it messes up the whole race. Same goes for supply chains. One error can result in delays or lost products. Because blockchain records every transaction in a way that's secure and transparent, errors can be spotted and fixed much faster.

Eliminating Fraud: Counterfeit goods are a massive problem. They can be dangerous (imagine fake medicine) and cost companies billions of dollars. With blockchain, it would be a lot easier to verify the authenticity of products. If a product's history can be tracked from start to finish, it's much harder for fakes to enter the supply chain.

Environmental and Ethical Impact: Some companies claim their products are "sustainably sourced" or "ethically made." But how do you know for sure? With blockchain, you could trace the entire life cycle of a product to see if it really lives up to those claims.

Cost-Effectiveness: All these benefits don't just make supply chains better; they can also make them cheaper. Fewer errors and faster shipments mean companies can save money, and hopefully, those savings get passed on to you.

You might be thinking, "Okay, but I'm not a business owner. Why should I care?" Here's the thing: improving supply chains has a ripple effect. It makes products safer, reduces waste, and can even help protect the environment. So while it might seem like a topic for businesspeople in suits, it actually matters to all of us.

And let's not forget, the journey from raw material to finished product involves many people—farmers, factory workers, truck drivers, and more. Better supply chain management can make their jobs easier and more secure, and that's a win for everyone.

Blockchain technology isn't just changing the way we deal with money; it's changing the way we interact with the physical world. The things you buy, the food you eat, even the gifts you give—they all have a story to tell. And with blockchain, that story becomes clearer, easier to follow, and a lot more trustworthy.

So the next time you pick up a product, remember: it's not just an item; it's a journey. And that journey is becoming more transparent, more efficient, and more ethical, thanks to blockchain.

7.3 Healthcare

When you're sick or hurt, the one thing you want most is to get better, fast. You depend on doctors, nurses, and a whole team of healthcare professionals to figure out what's wrong and how to fix it. But what if I told you that the healthcare system, a place that should be about healing and trust, is often tangled up in problems like paperwork errors, prescription mix-ups, and even fraud? It's a hard pill to swallow, but it's true.

Now, let's imagine a world where healthcare is more like a well-oiled machine and less like a maze you can't escape. Enter blockchain, the unsung hero that might just revolutionize the healthcare industry.

Patient Records: Imagine going to a doctor for the first time, and they already have all your medical history, securely and accurately stored. No more filling out endless forms, repeating your issues, or worrying that something important might be overlooked. With blockchain, your medical records could be stored in a secure, unchangeable system that any authorized doctor can access. This isn't just convenient; it can be life-saving in emergencies.

Drug Traceability: Counterfeit medicine is a grim reality. Fake drugs can be useless at best and deadly at worst. But with blockchain, every pill, vial, and syringe could be traced back to its original source. You'd know your medicine is real, safe, and effective.

Research and Trials: Finding new cures and treatments involves tons of data and many years of research. Sometimes, important information gets lost or misunderstood along the way. With blockchain, every piece of data is securely recorded and easily shared among researchers, making it easier to collaborate and discover new solutions to medical problems.

Insurance and Billing: Ever looked at a medical bill and thought, "What on Earth does this mean?" You're not alone. Medical billing is notoriously complicated. With blockchain, the entire process could be simplified. Everything, from the services you received to the amount your insurance covers, could be transparently and unchangeably recorded. This means fewer errors and faster payments.

Telemedicine: As remote doctor visits become more common, especially after the world experienced a pandemic, the question of how to keep these online interactions secure is crucial. Blockchain can encrypt and secure these digital appointments, making sure your personal information stays personal.

Data Security: You've probably heard of data breaches where hackers steal sensitive information. In healthcare, data security is even more critical. Your medical records are as personal as it gets, and blockchain's high level of security could protect that information from unauthorized access.

Global Healthcare: Right now, healthcare can be vastly different depending on where you are in the world. Blockchain could create a global standard, making quality healthcare more accessible for people everywhere. Imagine a world where no matter where you are—be it a small town or a big city, in a rich country or a poor one—you have access to the same level of healthcare.

We've come a long way in medicine. We've eradicated diseases, extended life expectancies, and improved the quality of life for millions. But the systems around healthcare—the red tape, the administration, the logistics—are lagging behind. They're stuck in the past, and they're dragging us down.

Blockchain offers a way to bring healthcare into the future. And this isn't just about making things easier or more convenient—though it does that too. It's about saving lives, preventing errors, and making sure everyone gets the care they deserve. The stakes are high, and that's exactly why getting it right matters so much.

So the next time you find yourself in a doctor's office or a hospital, remember: there's a silent revolution happening in the background, one that aims to make the healthcare system better, safer, and more efficient for everyone involved. And that's a prescription for change we can all get behind.

7.4 Voting and Governance

Alright, let's get serious for a moment. Voting is one of those things that many people take for granted, but it's actually a big deal. Why? Because it's how we make choices in our communities, cities, states, and even our entire country. But here's the kicker: the system we use for voting, like many other things in life, isn't perfect.

You've probably heard grown-ups grumble about long lines at voting stations, confusing ballots, or even worse, the fear that someone could mess with the votes. It's a situation that's as complicated as a Rubik's Cube and just as hard to solve. Or is it? That's where blockchain comes in, offering us some clever tools to make voting more secure, transparent, and maybe even a little easier.

Security: Imagine you had a diary that automatically locked itself if someone tried to tamper with it. That's somewhat how blockchain works. It's a record-keeping system so secure that once something is written in it, that 'something' can't be changed without leaving a trace. In the world of voting, this is a game-changer. No more worrying about rigged elections or tampered votes. If someone tries to cheat, blockchain will catch them red-handed.

Transparency: One of the big issues in voting is making sure everything is done fairly and openly, so everyone can trust the results. Blockchain can help with that too. Think of it like this: what if there was a transparent box at the voting station where you could see everyone's votes without knowing who voted for what? Blockchain can make the entire voting process that transparent, minus showing who voted for whom, of course.

Accessibility: Ever been stuck in a line, like at a theme park, and wished you could just skip ahead? Now, imagine standing in a line for hours just to vote. Not fun, right? With blockchain, there's a chance we could make secure digital voting possible, so you could vote from the comfort of your home. This would be especially helpful for people who can't easily get to voting stations, like the elderly or those with disabilities.

Real-Time Results: Waiting for voting results can be like waiting for the last episode of your favorite TV show — the suspense is unbearable! Blockchain could speed this up by providing real-time, reliable data as soon as votes are cast.

Reducing Costs: Setting up voting stations, printing ballots, hiring staff—all of this costs money. Lots of it. Blockchain could reduce these costs by simplifying the process, making it both more efficient and more secure.

Global Governance: It's not just about voting for the leader of your country. Blockchain could also be used for smaller-scale votes, like community projects or local laws. And it could even be used in other countries to help them set up more secure voting systems.

Imagine a world where every vote counts, really counts, because it's secure and transparent. Where people feel confident about the choices they make and trust the systems that record those choices. Where the maze of problems around voting finally gets untangled.

Blockchain isn't just a fad or a buzzword; it's a tool that can fix real-world problems. And when it comes to voting and governance, it might just be the secret ingredient we've been missing to make things run smoother, ensuring that everyone's voice is heard and counted.

So the next time you hear someone say, "My vote doesn't matter," you can tell them that changes are coming. Technologies like blockchain are working behind the scenes to make voting better, fairer, and more secure. And that's not just good governance; it's a step toward a better future for all of us.

7.5 Real Estate

Now, let's switch gears and talk about something most people only think about when they're grown up—buying a house. But you don't have to be a grown-up to understand why real estate is a big deal. It's not just about having a place to live; it's also about owning a piece of land or a building, which is often worth a lot of money.

Think of real estate like a game of Monopoly. You buy properties, trade them, or maybe even collect rent from other players. But unlike Monopoly, real estate transactions in real life are incredibly complex. There are heaps of paperwork, middlemen like agents and lawyers, and a long, winding process that can take months to complete. What if there was a way to simplify it all? Yep, you guessed it—enter blockchain.

Streamlining Transactions: Usually, buying or selling a property involves filling out stacks of forms and signing documents that you might not even understand. It's like having to complete a jigsaw puzzle with 1,000 pieces when you don't even know what the final picture should look like. Blockchain can cut through this clutter by digitizing all these papers and making the process much faster and clearer.

Transparency: Remember when you traded Pokémon cards or stickers with friends, and you could see exactly what you were getting? That's how blockchain can make real estate transactions transparent. Every step, from the first offer to the final sale, can be seen by everyone involved. It's a way to build trust, and when you're dealing with something as big as buying a house, trust is key.

Security: Just like in the voting system we discussed earlier, blockchain is super secure. Once a transaction is made, it's recorded in a way that can't be tampered with. This is crucial in real estate, where a small mistake or dishonest move can cost a fortune. Imagine if someone tried to sell you a house they didn't actually own! With blockchain, scams like this could be spotted instantly.

Smart Contracts: Imagine if your Monopoly game could automatically pay you rent when someone lands on your property. Blockchain can do something similar through 'smart contracts.' These are like regular contracts but smarter. They can automatically execute actions, like transferring property ownership, as soon as the conditions in the contract are met. So, no need for extra steps or middlemen.

Tokenization: This is a bit of a big word, but it's a neat idea. Imagine if you could buy a small piece of a really expensive building, like owning just one room in a skyscraper. That's what tokenization allows you to do. It breaks down property into smaller, more affordable pieces, making it easier for regular folks to invest in real estate.

Reducing Costs: Remember all those middlemen—agents, lawyers, banks? They all take a cut, making real estate more expensive for everyone. Blockchain can help reduce these costs by taking on some of these roles itself, like verifying transactions.

Global Opportunities: Real estate isn't just a local game; it's a global one. But buying property in another country comes with its own set of headaches, like different laws and currency issues. Blockchain can make this easier by creating a universal system that everyone understands and trusts.

Real estate might seem far away from your life right now, but it's a part of the adult world that nearly everyone has to deal with eventually. And whether you grow up to be a buyer, a seller, or even just a renter, blockchain could make that world a lot less confusing and more fair for everyone involved.

So, when you're old enough to think about buying your first house, you might find that the process isn't as scary or complicated as it sounds today. And that's because blockchain is working behind the scenes to clean up the mess and pave the way for a smoother, simpler future in real estate.

7.6 Beyond Currency

By now, we've talked a lot about how blockchain is shaking things up in various industries—from making your money more secure to helping doctors share medical records. But let's go one step further. Can blockchain really make a difference outside the world of money and business? You bet it can.

Environmental Impact: You know how superheroes in comics clean up the mess made by supervillains? Blockchain can be a sort of digital superhero for the environment. It can help track how much waste companies are producing, or how responsibly they are using natural resources. This way, companies can't just say they're "going green"; they'd have to prove it on a public and unchangeable record.

Education: Ever had a hard time proving you're good at something because you lost a certificate or diploma? With blockchain, your academic records can be stored in a secure, tamper-proof system. This means you can easily prove your qualifications to anyone, anytime. No more digging through old boxes for that kindergarten graduation certificate!

Art & Music: Piracy is a big issue for artists and musicians. People sometimes download music or art without paying for it, which is unfair to those who created it. Blockchain can help by tracking who owns what, making sure artists get paid when their work is bought or used.

Identity and Passports: Losing an ID or passport is a nightmare. And if someone steals it? Even worse. But what if your identity was securely stored on a blockchain? It would be like having a super-secure digital ID that's almost impossible to fake or steal.

Social Networks: Imagine a social network where you control all your own data, instead of the company that runs the site. Blockchain could make that happen. You decide who sees your photos, your posts, and your personal information. It would be like building a digital fortress around your online life.

Charity: Donating to charity is great, but how do you know your money is really going to a good cause? With blockchain, you can track every cent you donate, ensuring it goes exactly where it's supposed to. No more wondering if you're actually helping or if your money is just getting lost in the shuffle.

Food Safety: Ever wonder where your food comes from? Blockchain can track the journey of a product, from the farm to your table. This can help catch contaminated or unsafe food before it gets to you, which is definitely something to be thankful for.

Job Market: Finding a job is tough, and employers also struggle to find the right person for a job. Blockchain can make the match easier by storing accurate, verified information about job seekers and job openings. It's like a dating app, but for jobs!

Virtual Reality: As virtual worlds become more popular, they're starting to have their own economies, with digital land and goods to buy and sell. Blockchain could play a role in making sure these transactions are safe and fair, just like in the real world.

In the end, the possibilities for blockchain go far beyond what we've talked about. It's not just a one-trick pony; it's more like a Swiss Army knife of digital tools. It has the power to transform not just industries, but entire aspects of our daily lives, making them more secure, transparent, and fair.

So the next time you hear someone say that blockchain is just for cryptocurrencies, you'll know better. It's a game-changer, a digital revolution that has the potential to make the world a better place in so many ways.

And you're part of it. By understanding blockchain, you're not just ahead of the game; you're also better prepared for a future that's coming at us fast, ready or not. So keep watching, because the story of blockchain is far from over.

7.7 Key Takeaways

We've traveled quite a distance in this chapter, exploring the reaches of blockchain beyond the familiar realm of money and business. Let's wrap things up by highlighting some of the most crucial points:

Not Just About Money: Blockchain isn't only a tool for financial services. It has the ability to affect various sectors of our life and can be a powerful force for change in multiple industries.

Environmental Benefits: Companies can't just talk the talk about being environmentally friendly; blockchain can make them walk the walk by tracking waste and natural resource usage.

Educational Credentials: Blockchain can securely store your academic records, making it easy to prove your qualifications. Gone are the days of losing or damaging important certificates.

Protecting Artists: In the realms of art and music, blockchain helps to enforce ownership rights and ensure creators are compensated for their work.

Identity Safety: The technology has the potential to make identity theft incredibly difficult, storing your ID and passports securely on a blockchain.

User-Controlled Social Networks: Imagine a world where you control your own data on social media platforms. Blockchain could turn this into a reality.

Transparent Charity: Your charitable donations can be tracked to make sure they go exactly where they are intended, increasing trust in philanthropic activities.

Food Safety: From farm to table, blockchain can follow the journey of your food, helping to ensure that what you consume is safe.

Employment Solutions: Blockchain can hold verified information about job seekers and employers, streamlining the hiring process for both parties.

Virtual Realities: As we spend more time in digital spaces, blockchain ensures that transactions within these realms are just as secure as those in the real world.

By now, you should see that blockchain isn't a one-size-fits-all gadget; it's a versatile tool that can be adapted for numerous applications, each one potentially revolutionary in its own right. So, the next time someone tells you blockchain is just about cryptocurrencies, you'll have quite a few counterarguments up your sleeve.

And remember, the blockchain revolution is still in its early stages. Its potential is vast, and we've only begun to scratch the surface. Keep an eye on this evolving technology; it's a story that's far from over.

Part IV: Getting Started With Cryptocurrencies

Section 8: How to Buy Cryptocurrency

So you've ventured through the winding roads of cryptocurrency and blockchain. You've discovered how they were born, how they've evolved, and how they're more than just digital money. You've even realized that this is not just a story about technology, but also a story about people—people who dream, people who build, and people who dare to shake things up.

But now comes a very practical question: How do you actually buy cryptocurrency?

This is where the digital rubber meets the internet road, so to speak. Up until now, you might have thought of cryptocurrency as something abstract, something distant. It's like reading about the Amazon Rainforest but never setting foot in it. Buying cryptocurrency is the step that takes you from spectator to participant in this ongoing saga.

And let's be honest, it can feel a little intimidating. You're not just buying a candy bar from the store. You're stepping into a new financial world. A world that talks in codes, runs on decentralized networks, and operates 24/7. You'll be dealing with wallets but not the leather kind, with keys but not the metal kind, and with exchanges but not the kind you might have done if you've ever traveled to another country and had to swap dollars for euros or yen.

But fear not. We'll guide you through this in a way that won't make your head spin. And hey, you're not alone. Thousands of people step into the world of cryptocurrency every day. It's like the first day at a new school; everyone's a little nervous, but soon enough, you know your way around.

The process involves some key steps: choosing where to buy, knowing what you're buying, securing your purchase, and then actually making the transaction. Sounds simple enough, but each step has its own challenges and decisions to make.

Choosing where to buy, for instance, will introduce you to a place called a 'cryptocurrency exchange.' Think of it like a stock market, but for cryptocurrencies. There are also 'peer-to-peer' platforms where you buy directly from another person. Each option has its own set of pros and cons.

Knowing what you're buying means understanding that not all cryptocurrencies are the same. Just as you'd research before investing in stocks, you'll need to do some homework here, too. You can't just jump into the deep end without knowing how to swim, or in this case, without knowing the basics about the cryptocurrency you're interested in.

Securing your purchase will get you acquainted with 'cryptocurrency wallets.' These are like your personal cryptocurrency bank accounts but with added layers of security. They store your precious coins and keep them safe from online bandits.

And finally, making the transaction. This is where it all comes together. You'll pull the trigger and make your first buy. But don't worry, we'll be with you each step of the way.

So strap in. This part of the journey could change your financial landscape forever. It will empower you with the knowledge and tools to take part in a new economic future. But just as with any financial decision, it's important to tread carefully. There are risks and there are rewards, and understanding both is crucial.

Ready? Let's turn the page and step into the world of buying cryptocurrency.

8.1 Exchanges

Alright, folks, let's dig into the heart of buying cryptocurrency: exchanges. Think of an exchange like a marketplace—a buzzing, complex place where you can buy and sell all sorts of items. Except here, what's for sale isn't fruits or gadgets; it's cryptocurrency.

The First Exchanges: A Brief History

You can't really grasp the whole picture of exchanges without a bit of history. The story starts with Bitcoin. It was the first cryptocurrency, remember? Well, for a while, if you wanted Bitcoin, you had to mine it yourself. Imagine having to build your own car just to drive to the grocery store. But as interest grew, people started thinking, "Hey, why not create a place where we can simply trade these digital coins?"

And thus, the first Bitcoin exchanges were born. These were simple, rudimentary even. They looked nothing like the bustling hubs we have today. Think of it as going from a small roadside stand to a full-fledged mall. One of the earliest exchanges was called Mt. Gox, and it took off like a rocket. But it also crashed like one. Due to poor security and management, Mt. Gox ended up losing a lot of people's money. That was a lesson for the industry: security matters.

Types of Exchanges

Fast-forward to today, and you'll find several types of exchanges, each with its own style and set of rules.

1. **Centralized Exchanges (CEXs):** These are the big guys—places like Coinbase, Binance, and Kraken. They're called "centralized" because they act as the middleman for all transactions. It's a bit like a traditional bank. You trust them with your money, and they handle all the nitty-gritty details.

They're user-friendly but remember, they control your assets until you move them to your own wallet.
2. **Decentralized Exchanges (DEXs):** These are the rebels of the exchange world. Platforms like Uniswap and PancakeSwap let users trade directly with each other. No middleman, no central authority. It's more private and you have complete control over your assets. But it's also a bit like the Wild West—more freedom but more risks.
3. **Peer-to-Peer (P2P) Exchanges:** Imagine wanting to trade baseball cards with someone. You'd meet up, show your cards, and make a trade. That's P2P, but with cryptocurrency. Websites like LocalBitcoins act as a meeting ground but don't handle the money themselves.
4. **Futures Exchanges:** These are for the more experienced folks. Instead of buying cryptocurrency, you're making bets on its future price. It's high-risk, high-reward, and not recommended for beginners.

What to Look For in an Exchange

Choosing an exchange is a bit like choosing a school. You'll have to think about what matters most to you. Here are some key points to consider:

1. **Security:** Given the rocky history, security is your top priority. Look for exchanges that have strong security measures, like two-factor authentication (2FA) and cold storage for funds.
2. **Fees:** Exchanges make money by charging fees. Some are more affordable than others. Always read the fine print.
3. **User Interface:** If you're new to the game, you want an exchange that's easy to use. A complicated interface can lead to costly mistakes.
4. **Available Coins:** Not all exchanges offer all coins. If you have a specific cryptocurrency in mind, make sure the exchange you choose actually offers it.

5. **Customer Support:** If things go wrong—and they sometimes do—you want quick and helpful support.
6. **Regulation:** Some exchanges follow financial regulations to ensure they're on the up-and-up. This can offer an added layer of protection but can also limit some features.

The Risks

Buying cryptocurrency is like investing in anything else: it comes with risks. But the risks with exchanges can be unique.

1. **Hacking:** Despite advances in security, exchanges still get hacked. Always move your cryptocurrencies to your own secure wallet.
2. **Scams and Fraud:** Not all exchanges are honest. Some are set up to steal your money. Always do your research.
3. **Regulatory Risks:** Governments are still figuring out how to regulate cryptocurrency. An exchange that's legal today might face issues tomorrow.
4. **Technical Risks:** Glitches can happen. Imagine an exchange freezing up during a crucial trading moment. It's rare but possible.
5. **Liquidity Risks:** An exchange needs to have enough activity to ensure you can buy and sell when you want. Some smaller exchanges may not offer this liquidity.

In Summary

Exchanges are your gateway into the world of cryptocurrency. They've come a long way from their early, often chaotic, days. Whether you opt for a centralized, decentralized, or peer-to-peer approach will depend on your needs, your level of expertise, and your appetite for risk.

Remember, this is your money we're talking about. Exercise the same caution you'd use in any other financial venture. Research your options, understand the risks, and always be prepared for the unexpected.

In this arena, knowledge is your armor and caution is your shield. So equip yourself well as you step into the bustling, ever-changing marketplace of cryptocurrency exchanges.

8.2 P2P Transactions

All right, buckle up. We're diving into another chapter, and this one is going to be a fun ride. It's time to dig into Peer-to-Peer transactions, better known as P2P. You might think of this as the "secret handshake" of the crypto world, but don't worry, there's no secret password needed. Let's break it down.

Imagine you're trading baseball cards with your friends. You give them a card, and they give you one back—no middleman, just a straightforward swap. That's the essence of P2P transactions in cryptocurrency.

Now, let's take a step back. In the early days of Bitcoin, it was just a bunch of computer geeks sending coins back and forth. But as Bitcoin got popular, people wanted a more organized way to trade, so exchanges came into the picture. Think of these exchanges like big online marketplaces. They're awesome, but sometimes you want a more direct way to trade, like in the good old days. That's where P2P comes in.

In a P2P transaction, you're essentially doing a direct trade with someone else. No need for a middleman or an exchange to step in.

You find someone who wants to sell their Bitcoin, agree on a price, and boom! The Bitcoin is transferred from their wallet to yours.

This sounds great, right? Well, it is, but it's not without its dangers. You have to be really careful when you're doing P2P transactions. Why? Because you're relying on the other person to be honest and send you the Bitcoin after you've paid them.

That's why many people use P2P platforms. These are websites designed to make P2P trading safer. They work like an escrow service, holding onto the Bitcoin until both parties have done their part. Once the money has been transferred, the platform releases the Bitcoin to the buyer. This is a safer way to do P2P, but even then, you have to be cautious. Always check the reviews and ratings of the person you're trading with.

Now, you might be thinking, "Why would I want to go through all this when I can just use an exchange?" Well, exchanges are great, but they have fees and sometimes, limitations. P2P allows you more freedom and often lower fees, but it does come with higher risks.

Long ago, the first-ever Bitcoin transaction between two people took place. It was a P2P exchange. A guy named Laszlo Hanyecz paid 10,000 Bitcoins for two pizzas. Yep, you read that right—10,000 Bitcoins for two pizzas. Today, that would be worth a mind-boggling amount of money.

So, from buying pizzas to trading thousands of dollars worth of Bitcoin, P2P has come a long way. It's a piece of the crypto world that embraces the original spirit of digital currencies—freedom from middlemen and direct transactions.

But remember, the crypto world is a bit like the Wild West. It's a land of opportunities, but also full of risks. So, before you dive into P2P transactions, do your research, understand the risks, and maybe practice your secret handshake—just for good measure.

There you have it—a deep dive into the world of P2P transactions. It's a bit like going back to the roots of crypto while also stepping into the future. Just make sure you tread carefully, and you might find that P2P transactions offer just the kind of freedom and flexibility you've been searching for in the world of cryptocurrency.

8.3 ATMs

Ah, ATMs. You've probably used one before to get cash out of your bank account. They're on almost every corner, in convenience stores, and even at the mall. But did you know there are special ATMs just for cryptocurrency? Yep, that's right, and in this chapter, we're going to talk all about them.

First, let's make sure we're clear about what an ATM is. The term stands for Automated Teller Machine. These machines usually spit out paper money, but a crypto ATM is a little different. Instead of giving you dollars or euros, a crypto ATM can give you Bitcoin, Ethereum, or other types of digital money. Or, it can take your regular money and turn it into cryptocurrency for you.

So, why would anyone use a crypto ATM? Good question. These ATMs offer convenience. Let's say you're walking down the street and you suddenly decide you want to buy some Bitcoin. You can do it right then and there, no need to log into an online exchange or go through a lengthy sign-up process.

Now, don't get too excited just yet. While crypto ATMs are pretty cool, they come with their own set of challenges. For one, the fees can be high. Really high. Sometimes you'll have to pay up to 10%

more than you would on a regular online exchange. Why so much? Well, the people who operate these ATMs have to make money somehow, and those fees are their bread and butter.

Another thing to think about is security. Just like regular ATMs, crypto ATMs can be a target for thieves. Imagine if someone figured out how to hack into the machine. Your hard-earned money could be at risk. That's why it's important to use ATMs from reputable companies and in safe locations. Oh, and always, ALWAYS, double-check the address you're sending your crypto to. One wrong letter or number and your money could be lost in the digital abyss.

You also have to consider regulations. Cryptocurrency is still a bit like the Wild West, and different places have different rules. Some countries have outlawed crypto ATMs altogether, while others have embraced them with open arms. In the United States, for example, you'll probably need to show a government-issued ID before you can use one of these machines. It's all part of the effort to make sure people aren't using cryptocurrency for illegal activities.

And while we're on the subject of legality, let's talk about taxes. Yes, the taxman cometh, even in the world of cryptocurrency. Using a crypto ATM might make it harder to keep track of your transactions, which you'll need to do for tax purposes. So, keep your receipts, make a note, do whatever you have to do to make sure you're staying on the right side of the law.

The first crypto ATM appeared in Vancouver, Canada, in 2013. Since then, they've been popping up all over the world. Today, there are thousands of these machines, each one serving as a tiny outpost on the frontier of digital finance.

So, there you have it, the ins and outs of crypto ATMs. They offer quick and convenient access to the world of digital money, but they're not without their downsides. High fees, security risks, and the ever-watchful eye of Uncle Sam mean you'll need to tread carefully.

Still, in a world that's becoming more digital by the day, crypto ATMs represent another step toward a future where physical cash might be a thing of the past. Just remember, whether you're getting money from a machine on the corner or from a computer on the other side of the world, you need to know what you're getting into. Be smart, be safe, and you'll be just fine.

8.4 Key Takeaways

Alright, let's pause for a moment and go over the key points you should remember from this section about buying cryptocurrency. It's a lot to take in, but understanding these highlights will give you a solid base for stepping into the crypto world.

Exchanges: Online exchanges are the most common place to buy and sell cryptocurrencies. They offer a wide range of options but come with their own risks, like hacking and fraud. Always choose a reputable exchange and enable all security measures like two-factor authentication.

P2P Transactions: Peer-to-peer transactions let you buy or sell crypto directly with someone else. It's like a digital handshake, but be cautious. Always use a trusted platform to facilitate the trade, and remember, the risk of getting scammed is higher.

ATMs: Cryptocurrency ATMs offer the convenience of buying crypto on the go. However, they usually come with high fees, sometimes up to 10% more than online exchanges. Make sure to use ATMs from reputable providers and in safe locations.

Regulations and Taxes: The world of cryptocurrency is still like the Wild West in some ways, and laws can vary by country. In some places, you'll need to show ID to use a crypto ATM. And don't forget, you have to report your transactions for tax purposes.

Security: Whether you're using an exchange, doing a P2P transaction, or using an ATM, security should be your top concern. Use all available security features, double-check addresses, and keep records of your transactions.

Fees: Different methods of buying crypto come with different fees. Online exchanges usually offer the lowest fees, but even there, costs can vary. Always be aware of how much you're paying in fees as they can eat into your profits.

The Importance of Due Diligence: Always research before diving in. Whether it's choosing an exchange or deciding on a specific cryptocurrency to invest in, the more you know, the better equipped you'll be to make smart decisions.

The History Matters: The first crypto ATM was set up in 2013 in Vancouver, Canada. Knowing a bit about how these technologies came to be can give you a deeper understanding of the market today.

These are your survival basics, the knowledge you need to step into the world of cryptocurrency with confidence. Keep these points in mind, and you'll be off to a good start.

Section 9: Setting Up a Crypto Wallet

Welcome to Section 9, where we venture into the intriguing world of crypto wallets. If you're sitting there wondering what a crypto wallet actually is, don't worry; you're not alone. A wallet in the cryptocurrency universe is not made of leather or fabric, but it is as essential as the one you carry in your pocket.

Imagine you're a digital explorer, and you've just found a treasure—let's call it Bitcoin or Ethereum. You're excited, but here's the thing: you can't just put this treasure in your regular wallet or keep it under your mattress. It's digital, so you'll need a special digital wallet to hold it.

Cryptocurrency wallets are where you store your digital treasure. They come in various forms and serve as an essential gateway for any transactions you'll be making in the world of cryptocurrencies. You can think of them as high-tech safes that store your private keys—kind of like secret codes—that allow you to access your cryptocurrency.

In this section, we're going to delve deep into the different types of wallets you can use, each with its own pros and cons. We'll look at how you set up a wallet and secure it, which is of the utmost importance. Remember, losing access to your crypto wallet is like losing a treasure map. Except, in this case, there's no second map. It's gone for good.

You'll also discover that not all crypto wallets are created equal. Some are designed to be user-friendly but may lack advanced features. Others might be so secure that they require multiple steps just to access them. What's ideal for you will depend on what you need. Are you looking for something easy and quick to use, or are you in it for the long haul and looking for the safest, most secure option?

Before diving in, here are some terms you should get familiar with:

Private Keys: Think of these as your top-secret codes that give you access to your treasure. Never share these.

Public Address: This is like your email address for your wallet. People can send you cryptocurrencies to this address, but they can't take anything from you.

Seed Phrase: This is a series of words that you will use to recover your wallet if you forget your password or lose your device. Keep it safe, like a hidden treasure.

This section serves as your guide to choosing the best crypto wallet for your needs. Consider it your compass, steering you through the many options available and helping you avoid pitfalls. And trust me, there are many pitfalls: from wallets that are vulnerable to hacking to others that are so complicated they feel like you're cracking a code to get into a secret society.

The world of crypto wallets can seem complicated, but don't let that intimidate you. With a bit of guidance, setting up and using a crypto wallet can be as simple as setting up a new email account. But unlike an email account, a mistake can cost you. That's why it's crucial to understand how crypto wallets work and how to secure them.

By the end of this section, you'll be equipped with the knowledge you need to confidently use a crypto wallet, ensuring that your digital treasure is safe and accessible only by you. So tighten your seat belts, we're about to embark on an informative journey.

9.1 Types of Wallets

Alright, let's dig into the first major topic in this section: the different types of wallets you can use to store your digital treasures. Just like how you can keep your real-life money in various places—like a piggy bank, a safe, or a bank—cryptocurrency can be stored in different kinds of wallets, each with its own set of advantages and disadvantages.

Software Wallets

First up are software wallets, which are apps that you install on your computer or smartphone. These are sort of like digital piggy banks. They're easy to use and generally free. With a few taps or clicks, you can send or receive cryptocurrency. But just like you wouldn't store your life savings in a piggy bank, software wallets are not the most secure place to store large amounts of cryptocurrency. Why? Because if someone hacks into your computer or phone, they could get their hands on your digital treasure. Yikes!

Hardware Wallets

Next, we have hardware wallets. Think of these as your personal safes but for your digital assets. These are physical devices, like a USB stick, that you plug into your computer only when you need to make a transaction. The rest of the time, you keep it unplugged and in a safe place. Because it's not connected to the internet, hackers can't easily get to it. That's a big plus. But hardware wallets can be expensive, and if you lose the device, recovering your cryptocurrencies can be complicated.

Paper Wallets

Then there's the paper wallet, which is basically your crypto information printed out on a piece of paper. It's like having a treasure map that shows the location (public address) and the key (private key) to the treasure. Sounds simple, right? It is, but you have to be really careful with it. If you lose the paper or if it gets damaged (like if your dog decides it's a snack), your digital treasure is gone for good.

Online Wallets

Online wallets are another option. They're like keeping your money in a bank, except it's an online service that stores your cryptocurrency. Convenient, right? You can access it from any device, as long as you have an internet connection. But here's the downside: the online service has your private keys, and if they get hacked, you could lose your treasure.

Mobile Wallets

Mobile wallets are software wallets specifically designed for smartphones. They're really convenient for everyday transactions, like paying for a cup of coffee with Bitcoin. These wallets are easy to use, but again, not the safest for storing large amounts of cryptocurrency.

Desktop Wallets

Last but not least are desktop wallets. These are software wallets but for your computer. They offer a decent balance between ease of use and security. But remember, they're only as secure as your computer. If your computer gets infected with a virus or malware, your digital assets could be at risk.

What Should You Choose?

So, what type of wallet should you go for? Well, it depends on your needs. If you're just dipping your toes into the world of cryptocurrency and don't have much to store, a software wallet on your phone or computer might be good enough. But if you're planning to accumulate more digital treasure, you might want to invest in a hardware wallet or use a more secure online wallet.

Risk and Responsibility

Before we wrap up, let's talk a bit about risk and responsibility. Unlike regular money that's insured by the government, cryptocurrencies come with their own risks. There's no customer service hotline to call if you lose access to your crypto wallet. You're your own bank, and that comes with both freedom and responsibility.

Public and Private Keys

Your public address is like your account number, and your private key is like the most complicated password you've ever seen. Never share your private key. It's called 'private' for a reason.

Seed Phrases

Remember those seed phrases we talked about in the introduction? Write them down and keep them safe. If you lose access to your wallet, those seed phrases are your only way back in.

Final Words

Navigating through the types of crypto wallets may seem like a maze, but remember, the point of a maze is to find your way out. In this case, the "way out" is finding the wallet that's just right for you. It's like picking the perfect hiding spot for your most valuable treasure. So choose wisely, and take all the precautions you can. Your digital future might depend on it.

9.2 How to Set Up a Wallet

Setting up a crypto wallet might seem like a big, confusing project. But take a deep breath. We're going to break it down, step by step. By the end of this section, you'll know how to create your own digital vault for your cryptocurrency. Like any adventure, it's all about taking it one step at a time.

Step 1: Choose the Right Wallet for You

Remember all those types of wallets we talked about? Your first task is to pick one. If you're new to this world and don't have much cryptocurrency, a software wallet might be your best bet. It's like the beginner's level in a video game. But if you're holding a lot of digital treasure, consider a hardware wallet, the digital equivalent of a fortified castle.

Step 2: Download and Install

For software, mobile, and desktop wallets, this means going to the wallet's website and downloading the application. Always make sure you're on the official website. Scammers often set up fake sites to trick people. It's like falling into a trap in a treasure hunt—avoid at all costs.

For hardware wallets, you'll need to buy the device from a trusted retailer. Once it arrives, plug it into your computer to set it up.

Step 3: Create Your Wallet

Okay, you've downloaded the app or plugged in your hardware device. Now, it's time to set up your wallet. You'll usually see an option to create a new wallet. Click or tap on it.

Step 4: Set a Strong Password

Just like the lock on a treasure chest, your password is crucial. It's what stands between your digital assets and the outside world. Choose a strong password, something complicated with letters, numbers, and special characters. Write it down somewhere safe, but don't store it on your computer or phone.

Step 5: Backup Seed Phrase

After setting a password, you'll usually be given a seed phrase. This is a list of random words that act as a master key to your wallet. If you forget your password or lose access to your wallet, this is your way back in. Write down these words in the exact order they appear, and keep them somewhere extremely safe. Don't take a screenshot or save them on your computer; that's risky.

Step 6: Secure Your Backup

Remember that seed phrase? Make another copy and keep it in a different safe location. This is your ultimate backup. Some people even keep a copy in a safe deposit box at a bank.

Step 7: Activate Additional Security Measures

Most wallets offer extra security features like two-factor authentication, also known as 2FA. This is like having two locks on your treasure chest. Turn on all additional security measures available.

Step 8: Test It Out

Before you load all your treasure into your new digital vault, test it with a small amount. Send a tiny bit of cryptocurrency to your new wallet, and then try sending it back out to make sure everything is working correctly.

Step 9: Keep Your Software Updated

If you're using a software, mobile, or desktop wallet, keep it updated. Developers regularly release security updates. Ignoring these is like leaving your castle gates open.

Step 10: Monitor Your Wallet

Check in on your wallet regularly. If you notice any strange transactions or something seems off, take immediate action. Remember, in the world of crypto, you're your own security guard.

It's a Journey

Setting up a wallet is a journey, complete with challenges and decision points. But with each step, you're becoming more a part of the crypto world, a space full of opportunities and risks. Each type of wallet, each password, each security measure—they're all parts of your digital life. Like in any great story, the choices you make shape your experience.

Trust, But Verify

In the world of crypto, a saying to live by is "trust, but verify." Believe in the technology, but always double-check everything. From the website you're downloading your wallet from to the seed phrase backup, always be cautious.

Your Wallet, Your Responsibility

The freedom that comes with owning a crypto wallet also brings responsibility. There are no take-backs here. If you lose your password or seed phrase, your digital treasure could be lost forever. It's a sobering thought, but it's also empowering. You're in charge of your own digital destiny.

Final Words

The path to setting up your crypto wallet might seem winding and fraught with choices, but remember: every adventurer faces trials. Equip yourself with knowledge, be cautious, and make smart choices. Your wallet is more than a tool; it's your gateway to a new world of possibilities. So take the leap, set up your wallet, and start your journey. The digital world awaits.

9.3 Security Measures

In the world of crypto, security is more than just a buzzword. It's the fence that keeps your digital treasures safe. Imagine you've found the ultimate treasure—a chest full of sparkling gems and gold coins. You wouldn't just leave it out in the open, would you? Of course not. You'd want to lock it up tight, maybe hire some guards, and make sure nobody can get their hands on it without your say-so.

The Importance of Being Your Own Security

Cryptocurrency gives you a lot of freedom. There's no bank or government looking over your shoulder. But, just like a treasure hunter who has to watch out for traps and pitfalls, you're responsible for your own security.

Strong Passwords: Your First Line of Defense

Think of a strong password like the lock on a treasure chest. The more complicated the lock, the harder it is for thieves to open it. Use a mix of letters, numbers, and symbols. But make sure it's something you can remember—or write it down and keep it in a safe place.

Two-Factor Authentication: The Second Lock on the Chest

Two-Factor Authentication, or 2FA, adds an extra step to the login process. It's like having a second lock on your treasure chest. Even if someone guesses your password, they'll need a second code, usually sent to your phone, to get in. Activate 2FA wherever you can.

Seed Phrases: Your Master Key

We talked about seed phrases when setting up your wallet. Remember, they're like a master key that can open your wallet if you ever get locked out. Guard this phrase as you would your most valuable treasure.

Secure Backup: A Hidden Treasure Map

You wouldn't keep your treasure map out in the open for anyone to see, right? Same goes for your seed phrase and backup passwords. Some people write them down and keep them in a fireproof safe. Others might use a secure USB drive. Just make sure it's disconnected from the internet and hidden away.

Be Skeptical: Question Everything

In your crypto journey, you'll encounter all sorts of people and websites. Some will be friends; others will be traps. Just like in a treasure hunt, if something seems too good to be true, it probably is. Always double-check URLs to make sure you're on the real website, not a fake one set up to steal your information.

Software Updates: Keep Your Maps Current

Think of software updates like newer, more accurate treasure maps. They show you the safe paths and help you avoid newly discovered traps. Always update your wallet software and any security software you have.

Virtual Private Network: A Hidden Path

A Virtual Private Network, or VPN, is like a secret tunnel that helps you move more safely across the internet. It hides your location and encrypts your data. It's not a must-have, but it's a good extra layer of protection.

Cold Storage: The Ultimate Safe House

For the crypto you don't plan to spend or trade frequently, consider "cold storage," like a hardware wallet that's not connected to the internet. It's like hiding your treasure chest in a super-secret, underground vault.

Hardware Wallets: Fortresses and Castles

Hardware wallets are like fortresses or castles, the most secure places to store your treasure. They're immune to most online hacks because they're not connected to the internet. But you still have to keep them physically secure. Don't lose them, and don't let anyone else access them without your permission.

Monitoring: Always Keep Watch

Check your accounts regularly. If you see transactions you didn't make or anything else suspicious, act fast. The sooner you catch a problem, the better your chances of solving it.

Beware of Phishing: The Illusion Traps

Phishing is when scammers trick you into giving up your personal information. Be extra cautious with emails or messages that ask you to provide your password, seed phrase, or any other sensitive information.

Education: Knowledge Is Your Compass

The more you know, the better you'll be at staying safe. Read articles, watch videos, join forums—always keep learning. Even the most experienced treasure hunters keep updating their knowledge to stay ahead.

Your Team: A Trusted Circle

Surround yourself with people you trust and who know what they're doing. Even the most lone-wolf treasure hunters have a trusted team they can call on when things get tough.

Conclusion: The Never-Ending Journey

Security is a never-ending journey, full of twists and turns. There will always be risks and challenges, but also opportunities for those smart enough to take them. Keep your wits about you, stay updated, and never stop learning. Your digital treasures are worth protecting, and the adventure is yours to experience.

9.4 Key Takeaways

1. Be Your Own Security Guard: In the world of crypto, you're in charge of keeping your own "treasure" safe. There's no bank or big institution looking out for you.
2. Strong Passwords Matter: Think of your password like the lock on a treasure chest. The tougher it is, the harder for thieves to crack open your digital valuables.
3. Two-Factor Authentication (2FA): This is like adding a second, more complex lock to your treasure chest. Always turn it on when given the option.
4. Seed Phrases Are Essential: A seed phrase is like having a master key. It's crucial for recovering your assets if you ever lose access to your wallet. Keep it super safe.

5. Backup Wisely: Store your backup information like it's a treasure map: well-hidden, and well-protected.
6. Skepticism is Healthy: Always double-check and be cautious. If something seems too good to be true in the crypto world, it probably is.
7. Updates Are Your Friend: Keep your wallet and security software up-to-date. Think of it as getting the latest, most accurate treasure map.
8. Consider Using a VPN: A Virtual Private Network is like a secret tunnel, adding an extra layer of security when you're dealing with your digital treasures.
9. Cold Storage for Long-Term: If you're storing large amounts of crypto that you don't need immediate access to, consider cold storage like a hardware wallet.
10. Stay Informed: The crypto landscape is always changing, like a map that's being redrawn. The more you know, the better you can navigate it.
11. Phishing Traps Are Real: Always be cautious of fake emails or websites that try to steal your valuable information.
12. Team Up: Even the best adventurers need a reliable team. Surround yourself with trusted and knowledgeable people.

Remember, the adventure doesn't end here. Security is a constant journey. The better you get at it, the safer your treasures will be. Keep learning, keep questioning, and keep exploring. The world of crypto is vast and filled with both opportunities and challenges, but with the right tools, you can conquer it.

Section 10: Understanding Public and Private Keys

You've heard about treasure chests and maps, right? Well, in the world of cryptocurrency, the way you access your digital treasure isn't with a rusty old key or by following a faded, ink-splattered map. No, in this digital realm, you unlock your riches with something far more advanced yet infinitely more sensitive: keys. But not just any keys. We're talking about Public and Private Keys. Don't worry; there are no actual physical keys involved. These are strings of letters and numbers that hold the power to unlock your wealth. Yep, you heard right—strings of letters and numbers are what stand between you and your hard-earned digital coins.

Imagine for a moment you've found a treasure. But it's not just one chest; it's two. One chest is open for people to see what's inside, like the display window at a store. That's like your Public Key. It's what people can see and use to send you cryptocurrency. You share it openly, and it's part of how the blockchain keeps track of transactions. The more people you share this chest with, the more you can collect.

Now, what about the other chest? This one is secret. You only open it when you want to use what's inside or add more to it. This one is locked and only you should have the key. That's your Private Key. Unlike the Public Key, your Private Key is for your eyes only. If anyone else gets it, they have the power to open your secret chest and take everything inside. Scary, right?

So, why are these keys so important? They're the heart of blockchain security. Imagine them as gatekeepers. They decide who gets to add information to the blockchain, and who gets to own or transfer digital coins. Without them, there would be chaos. Anyone could claim any amount of money or change records as they please. It's like if, in a game of capture the flag, there were no rules about who could grab the flag or how. It would be complete madness. But thanks to these keys, everything stays in order.

In this section, we'll dive deep into the world of Public and Private Keys. We'll learn how they're created, how they work, and why they're so crucial for maintaining the order and security in the vast, complicated world of cryptocurrency. We'll explore how these keys function like digital signatures, adding a layer of security and authenticity to each transaction. We'll also delve into the dangers of losing your Private Key and how you can keep it secure, because remember, with great power comes great responsibility.

Don't underestimate the significance of understanding Public and Private Keys. While they may seem daunting at first, getting to know them is like unlocking a secret level in a video game. And the prize? A deeper, more secure experience in the exciting world of cryptocurrency. So grab your virtual explorer's hat, because we're about to dig into another major cornerstone of the crypto universe. And let me tell you, it's a cornerstone you'll want to understand. After all, what's the point of finding treasure if you can't keep it safe?

Are you ready to unlock the secrets? Let's go.

10.1 What They Are

Okay, explorers. You've just unlocked the door to one of the most crucial parts of the cryptocurrency puzzle: Public and Private Keys. Remember those treasure chests we talked about? Let's take a closer look at their "keys" and find out what makes them so special—and so important.

You might be wondering, "Are these keys like the passwords to my computer or my email?" Sort of, but they're even more powerful and way more specific. A password is like a single key that locks or unlocks one door. But in the crypto world, Public and Private Keys work together like a highly secure, one-of-a-kind lock and key system. It's like having a treasure chest that can only be opened by a magical key, and you're the only one who holds that magic.

Public Keys

First, let's talk about Public Keys. Imagine your Public Key as your mailbox. Anybody can drop a letter (or in this case, cryptocurrency) into it. It's your public address on the blockchain, and it's created from a chunk of mathematical data. Complicated, right? But don't worry. You don't need to understand the math to use it. All you need to know is that it's like your identity on the blockchain.

If someone wants to send you some cryptocurrency, you give them your Public Key. It's like saying, "Hey, here's the address to my mailbox. Drop the coins in when you're ready." Just like your home address, your Public Key is information that you can share openly. It's safe to do so because people can only use it to send you things, not take things away.

Private Keys

Now, onto Private Keys. These are the keys to the kingdom—or, should I say, the keys to your treasure chest. A Private Key is like a secret code that only you should know. It's created alongside your Public Key, but unlike the Public Key, this one is just for you. Your Private Key can unlock the transactions connected to your Public Key. In simpler terms, you use your Private Key to open your mailbox and take out the letters or coins people have sent you.

Here's where it gets critical. Your Private Key is the only way you can prove that you own the cryptocurrency linked to your Public Key. It's like the only copy of the magical key that opens your secret treasure chest. If someone else gets their hands on it, they can take everything. So, keep it locked up tighter than a drum.

Why Both?

You might be asking, "Why do I need both?" Great question. Your Public Key is what allows people to send you cryptocurrency. It's like how people need your email address to send you an email. But your Private Key is what lets you access and use those funds. You need both to complete the circle. One to receive, and the other to send or use.

It's like having a mailbox that everyone can put letters into (Public Key), and having the only key that can open that mailbox to take letters out (Private Key). The two keys work together, like a perfect team in a relay race. The Public Key receives, and the Private Key unlocks and uses.

So, let's get real. These keys aren't something to take lightly. They're not like an extra set of house keys that you can easily replace if you lose them. If you lose your Private Key, you lose access to your cryptocurrency. That would be like losing the key to your treasure chest forever. You can look at it, but you can't touch what's inside. Ever.

Understanding Public and Private Keys is like learning the rules of a new game. It might seem complicated at first, but once you get the hang of it, it'll become second nature. Just remember, with these keys in your pocket, you're not just a player. You're the keeper of your own digital destiny. So treat them with the respect they deserve.

Ready to journey on? Keep those keys close. We've got more secrets to uncover.

10.2 Why They Are Important

You've got the lowdown on what Public and Private Keys are. Now, let's venture into the 'why'—why they're such a big deal. Strap in, because this part of the journey takes us into the very heart of what makes cryptocurrency so unique, and so, so important.

The Heart of Security

Remember, your Private Key is like the magical key to your treasure chest. Lose that key, and your treasure—your cryptocurrency—will be locked away forever. Sounds dramatic, doesn't it? But it's not an exaggeration. In the real world, if you lose the key to your house, you can call a locksmith. In the cryptocurrency world, there's no locksmith that can bail you out. Your Private Key is your personal locksmith, and there's only one copy of it. So, yes, the stakes are high.

Identity in a Digital World

Now think about your Public Key. It's like your home address in the digital world of blockchain. Anyone who knows this address can send you cryptocurrency. In a way, your Public Key is a part of your digital identity. But unlike your real name or your email, it doesn't reveal who you are. It's a way to interact with people, make trades, and do business without revealing your entire life story. It's privacy and openness all wrapped into one.

The Power of Ownership

Let's dig a little deeper. Why do you think it's so important to have this level of control over your own assets? Before cryptocurrency and blockchain, the banks were the gatekeepers. They held your money, and they made the rules. You trusted them to keep your money safe, but you also had to play by their rules.

With Public and Private Keys, you become your own bank. Imagine that! You're not just keeping your money under your mattress; you're safeguarding it in a high-tech treasure chest that only you can open. You set the rules. It's an incredible level of financial freedom that people never had before. But remember, with great power comes great responsibility.

No More Middleman

In traditional transactions—let's say, buying a book online—there are a lot of steps and middlemen involved. Your payment goes through various banks and payment processors before it finally reaches the bookstore. And each one of these middlemen takes a piece of the pie. They charge fees, and they have access to your financial information. The more middlemen, the more risks and the more costs.

Your Public and Private Keys cut out these middlemen. It's just you and the other person, sending and receiving funds directly. It's faster, cheaper, and safer. But the catch is that you are solely responsible for the transaction. There's no customer service to call if things go wrong. Your keys, your responsibility.

A Network of Trust

Your keys play a huge role in making the blockchain a 'trustless' system. Wait, 'trustless'? Does that mean you can't trust it? Nope. It means you don't have to trust anyone else in the system because the system itself is designed to be secure. Your Public and Private Keys create a seal of authenticity on your transactions that's almost impossible to fake. So when someone receives a transaction from your Public Key, they can be 100% sure that it's legit and it's from you.

This system of Public and Private Keys is what makes cryptocurrency more than just a digital version of money. It's a revolution in how we think about and handle finance, identity, and trust. In this new world, you're not just a user; you're a guardian of your own destiny.

So, as you keep these keys, imagine them as more than just lines of numbers and letters. They're your sword and shield in the blockchain realm. A way to carve out your own space, protect your assets, and interact with a global network.

Yeah, it's that epic. Ready to move on? Keep those keys handy; the journey's far from over.

10.3 Key Takeaways

Alright, time to gather what we've learned in a neat little package. Understanding Public and Private Keys is like understanding the DNA of cryptocurrency and blockchain. It's the core that keeps this revolutionary system ticking, so here's what you should remember:

1. **The Heart of Security:** Your Private Key is the ultimate safeguard for your digital assets. Lose it, and you lose access to your cryptocurrency. No locksmiths in the blockchain world!
2. **Identity in a Digital World:** Your Public Key is like your address in the digital realm. It's a way to receive cryptocurrency and interact with people, all while keeping your real identity a mystery.
3. **The Power of Ownership:** Public and Private Keys put you in control. You become your own bank, setting the rules and enjoying an unprecedented level of financial freedom.

4. **No More Middleman:** These keys allow you to make direct transactions, cutting out the need for banks or other intermediaries. Fewer middlemen mean fewer fees and quicker transactions.
5. **A Network of Trust:** In a 'trustless' system like blockchain, your keys ensure the authenticity of your transactions. They make the network secure, so you don't have to trust anyone; you just trust the system itself.
6. **Great Power, Great Responsibility:** With the liberty these keys offer, comes an equally hefty responsibility. They are your duty to protect. If you're careless with them, the consequences can be severe.
7. **Revolution in Interaction:** The concept of Public and Private Keys has redefined how we think about financial transactions, identity, and trust on a fundamental level.

In the end, it's not just about keeping some codes safe; it's about understanding the transformative power you hold in your hands. With these keys, you're not just participating in a new form of currency; you're part of a paradigm shift in how the world handles money, identity, and trust.

So, keep these key takeaways in mind as you navigate the complex, yet thrilling world of cryptocurrency. There's much more to explore, and your keys are the ticket to that uncharted territory. Keep them safe, and the possibilities are endless.

Section 11: Cryptocurrency Mining

Imagine a world beneath our feet, teeming with treasure. Gold, diamonds, and rare minerals lie hidden, buried deep within the Earth's crust. Now, picture a bunch of prospectors and miners, armed with picks, shovels, and advanced machinery, working tirelessly day and night to unearth these treasures. They search for the hidden gems, not just for the thrill but for the value these gems hold. Every nugget they find brings them closer to striking it rich. But mining is not just about luck; it's a complex and intricate process that demands skill, effort, and an intimate understanding of the geology.

Now, shift that image from the world of soil and rock to the realm of computers and code. Welcome to the landscape of cryptocurrency mining. Just like gold miners, crypto miners are on a relentless quest. But instead of digging through dirt, they're sifting through complex mathematical problems. And instead of finding precious stones, they're rewarded with cryptocurrency.

At this point, you might be scratching your head, wondering how one can "mine" something that doesn't physically exist. Good question. You see, cryptocurrency, particularly Bitcoin, was designed with a "mining" process to create new tokens and validate transactions. The whole operation happens in a virtual world, but the rules of the game are as hard and fast as the laws of physics.

Mining is the backbone that keeps the cryptocurrency network alive and functioning. Miners use powerful computers to solve complex equations. When they crack the code, they add a 'block' to the 'chain,' thereby confirming a set of transactions. For their hard work, they receive a miner's fee and a small piece of a newly minted cryptocurrency. Sounds simple, but it's as complicated as any detective story filled with twists, turns, and unexpected challenges.

So why should you care about cryptocurrency mining if you're not planning on becoming a miner yourself? Well, understanding mining gives you a deeper insight into how cryptocurrencies work. It sheds light on the incredible innovation that goes into maintaining a decentralized network. You'll also learn about the real-world impact of mining, from the towering electricity bills to the heated debates on its environmental implications. Plus, if you ever decide to step into the world of crypto investment, knowing the ins and outs of mining can give you an edge.

The concept of mining will challenge your understanding of currency and transactions. It flips the script, turning your idea of money-making on its head. Forget about banks printing money; here, the miners are the creators and validators. They're the unsung heroes who keep the show on the road.

In this section, we'll journey through the labyrinthine world of cryptocurrency mining. You'll discover what it takes to be a miner, the kinds of mining that exist, and the hurdles miners have to overcome. It's not a story for the faint-hearted, but then again, neither is the entire world of cryptocurrency.

So grab your virtual pickaxes, fasten your seat belts, and prepare for an enlightening dive into the depths of cryptocurrency mining. Trust me; it's an expedition worth embarking upon. Let's dig in.

11.1 What is Cryptocurrency Mining?

Picture yourself in a giant library, one that holds the most important information of an entire city. There are countless books, neatly arranged in shelves, each containing unique stories, facts, and records. But there's one problem: new information keeps flooding in every second, and someone needs to organize it into new books and put those books on the shelves. That's not all; for each book you correctly place, you get a small but valuable reward. Sounds like an interesting job, doesn't it?

Welcome to the world of cryptocurrency mining—a job that's crucial but challenging, and absolutely central to the entire system of cryptocurrencies like Bitcoin, Ethereum, and many others. But instead of a physical library, miners work in a digital one, and instead of books, they're handling transactions—lots and lots of transactions.

How It All Begins

Let's start at the beginning. People all around the world are sending and receiving cryptocurrencies. Maybe someone in Japan is buying a new camera from a seller in Germany using Bitcoin. Or perhaps a person in Brazil is investing in a handful of Ethereum tokens. These transactions are like puzzle pieces, waiting to be connected to form a complete picture.

The Mining Process

Now, this is where the miners come into play. Using powerful computers, miners collect these pending transactions and place them into a 'block.' You can think of a block as a super-tough, locked treasure chest filled with transactions. But it's not just about throwing transactions into a block; miners have to solve an incredibly complex mathematical problem to lock this treasure chest securely. This problem is so hard that it would take even the fastest human years to solve it. But these computer systems, known as 'rigs,' can do it in about ten minutes.

The Reward System

Solving the mathematical problem and locking the treasure chest—err, the block—isn't just for fun. When a miner successfully solves the problem, they get to add that block to a long, ever-growing chain of similar blocks. This is known as the 'blockchain,' and it serves as the public ledger for all transactions in a given cryptocurrency. Once a block is added, it's there for good, providing a transparent and unchangeable record of transactions.

As a reward for their hard work, miners receive two things. First, they get a small, predetermined number of new cryptocurrency tokens—this is known as the 'block reward.' Second, they collect transaction fees from the users whose transactions were included in the new block. So, in a way, it's like they've been paid twice!

The Risks and Challenges

Sounds simple enough, right? Not so fast. Mining comes with its share of risks and challenges. First, it's a competitive field. Miners are racing against each other to solve the next problem and add the next block. Only the first one to solve it gets the reward. Others, who also may have spent the same amount of time and energy, walk away with nothing.

Second, the mathematical problems aren't just tough; they're designed to become more difficult over time. As more miners join the network and computers become more powerful, the problems adjust to keep the block-solving time relatively consistent.

And let's not forget the cost. Running powerful computers day and night consumes a lot of electricity, which means big utility bills. Not to mention, these mining rigs aren't cheap. A good setup can cost thousands of dollars, and there's no guarantee you'll 'strike gold' to make it all back.

Environmental Concerns

Last but not least, there's a growing debate about the environmental impact of cryptocurrency mining. Those powerful computers need a lot of energy, and if that energy comes from non-renewable sources like coal, it's not great for our planet. Some people argue that the environmental cost is too high for the benefits we get from cryptocurrencies.

The Unsung Heroes

Despite the hurdles, miners play a role as essential as that of doctors in a hospital or teachers in a school. Without miners, transactions would grind to a halt, and the whole cryptocurrency world would crumble. They're the unsung heroes, working behind the scenes to keep the system functioning smoothly. And although it's not a job without challenges, the miners believe in the value and future of cryptocurrencies. Just like pioneers in any field, they're taking risks and pushing boundaries, all in the hope of building something that will last.

So, the next time you hear the term 'cryptocurrency mining,' picture those digital miners, tirelessly solving puzzles to keep the cryptocurrency library in order. It's hard work, but someone's got to do it. And who knows, maybe one day, that someone could be you.

And there you have it: the complex, intriguing, and highly essential world of cryptocurrency mining explained. Now you know it's not just a simple dig-and-find treasure game. It's a critical job that keeps the cryptocurrency world ticking. But don't put away your pickaxe just yet; we've got more ground to cover. Stay tuned.

11.2 How Does It Work?

Alright, you've met the unsung heroes of the cryptocurrency world, the miners. Now, let's pull back the curtain and see how they do what they do. How do they manage to dig up these digital treasures? Let's break it down.

The Digital Pickaxe

To start, miners need a digital 'pickaxe,' and that comes in the form of a computer. But not just any old desktop or laptop will do. Miners use specialized computers with super-strong hardware to solve the complex puzzles that stand between them and a new block on the blockchain.

The Puzzle and the Lock

You remember how we compared each block to a treasure chest? Well, that chest is locked with a complex math problem. It's like a puzzle lock, and solving it requires a lot of computing power. This complex math problem is what miners strive to solve. It's known as 'Proof of Work,' and it's how the system makes sure that only the fastest and most accurate miner adds the next block.

Hash Functions

To solve the problem, miners use a technique called 'hashing.' Imagine you have a secret code, and you want to make sure it stays secret. Hashing takes that code and turns it into a jumble of numbers and letters. This jumbled mess, called a 'hash,' represents the original code but is almost impossible to decode back.

The challenge for miners is to find a specific hash that fits certain rules. Think of it as trying to find a key that fits a lock, except the key is made of numbers and letters, and the lock is a computer algorithm.

Mining Software

But miners don't work alone. They use specialized software to help them with their job. This software connects the miner's computer to the network of that specific cryptocurrency. It also provides a dashboard where miners can see the progress of their work, like a control room for a spacecraft. From there, they can adjust settings, check the status of their hardware, and even see how close they are to solving the current puzzle.

The Mining Pool

Mining is a competitive sport. It's like a race, where everyone is trying to solve the puzzle first. Because the competition is stiff, miners often join groups called 'mining pools.' In a pool, miners combine their computing power to solve puzzles faster. When one member of the pool wins, the reward is split among all members. It's a bit like a soccer team sharing a trophy.

Consensus Mechanism

Now, in any system where there's a competition, there need to be rules. In the world of cryptocurrency, this set of rules is called a 'consensus mechanism.' It's a way to make sure everyone agrees on which blocks are valid and which aren't. The most common consensus mechanism is the one we've been talking about: Proof of Work. But there are others, like 'Proof of Stake,' where the right to add a block is based on how many tokens you own, not how fast you can solve a puzzle.

Once a Block is Mined

So what happens when a miner finally solves the puzzle? First, the new block is added to the blockchain. This is the miners' ultimate goal: to expand that ever-growing public ledger with more secure, verified transactions. Once that's done, the miner receives their reward in the form of newly minted cryptocurrency tokens and transaction fees from the block they just sealed.

The Challenge of Scalability

With all this talk of racing to solve puzzles and add blocks, you might wonder how many transactions can actually fit in a block. The answer depends on the cryptocurrency. For Bitcoin, it's usually around 2,500 transactions. That may sound like a lot, but considering the millions of transactions that happen daily, it's a drop in the bucket.

This issue is called 'scalability,' and it's one of the most significant challenges in the cryptocurrency world. Developers are continually trying to make the system faster and more efficient, but it's like trying to add more lanes to a crowded highway; there's only so much room to expand.

The Balancing Act

Cryptocurrency mining is a delicate balance. Miners need to be fast but also accurate. They have to keep their equipment running smoothly, manage their electricity costs, and stay ahead in a highly competitive field. And let's not forget, the rules of the game can change. If too many people start mining, the puzzles can get harder, or the rewards might get smaller.

You see, there's more to mining than just solving puzzles and raking in digital coins. It's a complex system that demands a blend of skill, luck, and sheer computing power. It's not a get-rich-quick scheme, nor is it a casual hobby. It's a full-time job, often requiring 24/7 attention. For those who make a career out of it, mining is a labor of love. It has its fair share of frustrations and challenges, but the rewards—both literal and figurative—can be significant.

Mining might seem like an arcane subject, a mystery wrapped in numbers and algorithms. But it's essential to understand this process if you want to get to the heart of what makes cryptocurrencies tick. It's like understanding the engine that powers a car or the gears inside a watch. When you know how it works, you appreciate it all the more.

So there you have it. The next time you hear about Bitcoin's price shooting up or read a headline about cryptocurrency adoption, spare a thought for the miners. They're the ones keeping the digital gears turning, the unsung heroes of a revolutionary financial landscape.

And who knows, maybe you'll pick up a digital pickaxe one day and join the race. It's a tough gig, but for those who crack the code, the sky's the limit. Stay tuned, we've still got more to dig into.

11.3 Is It Profitable for Beginners?

So, you've learned what cryptocurrency mining is and how it works. Now, the burning question on your mind might be: "Can I make money doing this?" Well, it's not a simple yes-or-no answer. Like many things in life, it's complicated.

The Gold Rush Comparison

Remember those old stories about the Gold Rush? How people packed their bags and headed west, hoping to strike it rich by digging up gold? For a few lucky folks, that dream came true. But for many others, it was a tough journey filled with challenges. They had to buy equipment, fight off competitors, and dig countless holes, all for a chance to find something valuable.

Cryptocurrency mining can be a lot like that. The idea of earning money—possibly lots of it—just by letting a computer run some software sounds like a dream come true. But just like those gold miners from history, today's digital miners face their own set of challenges.

Start-Up Costs

First, let's talk about the initial costs. You'll need a computer, and not just any computer. Mining requires a powerful machine, often a specialized one built just for mining tasks. These computers are not cheap. We're talking about a range of thousands of dollars.

Then there's the electricity bill. Mining consumes a ton of power. Some miners find their electricity costs are higher than what they earn from mining. It's like using a giant net to catch fish but finding out the net costs more than the fish you catch.

Technical Knowledge

This isn't something you just jump into. You need a good understanding of how blockchain technology works, along with the specifics of mining algorithms. It's like learning a new language—one made up of numbers, codes, and computer jargon. The learning curve is steep.

Competition and Complexity

Remember, mining is a race. You're competing with other miners to solve a puzzle. The more people who join the race, the harder it gets to win. The puzzles become more complex, and the rewards are harder to grab. Long gone are the days when you could mine Bitcoin with a simple home computer. Now you're racing against supercomputers and entire warehouses filled with mining rigs.

Pooling Resources

To even the odds, many miners join 'mining pools' where they combine their computing power and split the rewards. But even this has its drawbacks. Pools often charge fees, and you still have to share the rewards with many other miners. It's like being part of a treasure-hunting team but having to split the treasure many ways.

Risk and Reward

Also, the value of cryptocurrencies can go up and down like a roller coaster. You might mine coins when they're not worth much and hope the price goes up. But there's no guarantee it will. It's a gamble, plain and simple.

Regulations and Laws

Let's not forget the rulebook. Cryptocurrencies are still relatively new, and governments are trying to figure out how to regulate them. You need to be aware of the laws in your country. In some places, mining might even be illegal.

Environmental Concerns

Lastly, there's the issue of environmental impact. All that electricity usage contributes to a larger carbon footprint. Some people are questioning the ethics of consuming so much energy for a digital activity. It's a hot topic, and if you're thinking about mining, it's something to consider.

What's the Verdict?

So, is cryptocurrency mining profitable for beginners? It can be, but it's not guaranteed. It requires a significant investment of time, money, and energy—both electrical and personal.

Don't expect to get rich quick. It's more like a marathon than a sprint, a long-term commitment that might pay off—or might not. You could compare it to starting a business; it's risky, demanding, and the market is highly competitive. But, like any business, it also offers the chance for significant rewards.

If you're tech-savvy, good with numbers, and willing to invest the time and resources, mining could be an exciting adventure into the world of cryptocurrency. Just remember, every adventure has its risks. It's crucial to do your homework and know what you're getting into. Equip yourself with the right knowledge and tools, and who knows, you might just strike digital gold.

For those who find the risk too high, or the technical aspects too challenging, there are other ways to get involved in the world of cryptocurrencies. You could trade coins, invest in blockchain startups, or even work for a company that deals in digital currencies.

So, to all aspiring miners out there, weigh your options carefully. Think hard, plan well, and if you decide to go for it, may your pickaxe always strike true.

11.4 Key Takeaways

1. **Initial Costs:** Mining is not free. It requires a significant upfront investment in specialized hardware and software. Expect to shell out a good chunk of money to get started.
2. **Electricity Expenses:** Mining eats up a lot of power. Sometimes the cost of electricity can outweigh the value of the coins you mine, essentially costing you more than you earn.
3. **Technical Skills Required:** You'll need a solid understanding of blockchain technology and mining algorithms. It's a field that demands technical know-how.
4. **Competition is Fierce:** The more people who mine, the harder it gets to earn rewards. You're essentially in a race

against many other miners, some of whom have extremely powerful machines.
5. **Mining Pools:** These are groups where miners combine their computing power to improve their chances of earning rewards. While this can increase your odds, remember that you'll have to share the rewards and possibly pay fees.
6. **Market Volatility:** The value of cryptocurrencies can fluctuate wildly. One day your digital coins might be worth a lot, and the next day, not so much. It's a gamble.
7. **Legal and Regulatory Risks:** Always be aware of the laws regarding cryptocurrency in your country. Regulations can change, and you need to be prepared for that.
8. **Environmental Concerns:** The high energy consumption associated with mining has environmental implications, contributing to a larger carbon footprint.
9. **Not a Get-Rich-Quick Scheme:** Profitability is not guaranteed. Like starting a business, it's a long-term commitment that can either pay off or leave you with less than you started with.
10. **Alternatives Exist:** If mining seems too risky or complicated, there are other ways to get involved in the cryptocurrency space, like trading or investing.

By now, you should have a clearer picture of what cryptocurrency mining entails, along with the risks and potential rewards. It's a complicated field, one that requires careful thought and planning. If you decide to dive in, make sure you're well-prepared for the journey ahead.

Part V: Investing & Trading

Section 12: Why Invest in Cryptocurrencies?

Imagine you're holding a map that could lead to a treasure. It's a puzzle, full of twists and turns, and you have to figure out if the treasure at the end is worth the quest. Welcome to the world of investing in cryptocurrencies. But, before you rush off, ready to dig up your digital gold, let's talk about what's on the line here.

Firstly, why are we even discussing investing in cryptocurrencies? You might have heard adults talking about traditional investments like stocks, bonds, and real estate. So what makes cryptocurrencies different, and why should they catch your attention?

Cryptocurrencies are not just digital money. They're part of a whole new financial landscape that's still being built, much like constructing a brand new city. Imagine building a city with no need for keys because every door recognizes you. A city where you don't have to worry about your money getting stolen, thanks to advanced encryption. A city where you are the one in control, not some big institution. That's the vision driving this digital world of cryptocurrencies.

Some people invest in cryptocurrencies to be part of this revolution. They believe this could be the future, and they want in, right from the start. Others are here for the profit. Prices of cryptocurrencies can go up and down like a roller coaster. Buy low, sell high—that's the game. But, it's not as simple as it sounds. The high volatility of these digital coins means they are risky investments. Yes, you could gain a lot, but you could also lose a lot. That's why it's crucial to understand what you're getting into.

You might wonder how different cryptocurrencies like Bitcoin, Ethereum, and Dogecoin are from each other. It's like comparing diamonds, gold, and silver. Each has its unique features and value, both in what it does and how people perceive it. We'll delve into these nuances later to give you a clearer picture.

Also, let's not forget the role of technology. Cryptocurrencies exist because of groundbreaking technology like blockchain. It's as if someone invented a magical ink that makes counterfeiting impossible, changing the way we think about money.

But beware! The world of cryptocurrencies is like a wild jungle with hidden pitfalls. There are no safety nets here. No government protections like you'd find with a regular bank. If you're careless, you could lose your investment to scams, hacking, or simple mistakes like losing your password. That's why one of the critical parts of this section is to arm you with knowledge to navigate these risks.

At the same time, don't let these warnings scare you away from a field that also offers immense possibilities. You could support projects that aim to change the world for the better or back technologies that could become the next big thing. Investing in cryptocurrencies can be about more than just making money. It can be about backing a vision, a dream of what the world could be.

So, are you ready to decode this map to potential treasure? This section will guide you through the compelling reasons why you might want to invest in cryptocurrencies and help you understand the risks and rewards awaiting you.

Hold tight; this is going to be an enlightening journey.

12.1 Potential for High Returns

So, you're still intrigued? That's the spirit! We've been talking about this new world of cryptocurrencies like it's a treasure hunt, but let's put on our detective hats for a moment. One big reason people even look at cryptocurrencies is the potential for high returns. In other words, they hope to make a lot of money. But why? What's the story behind this?

Imagine this: It's 2010, and you hear about this strange digital thing called Bitcoin. Most people laugh it off. It sounds like something out of a science fiction movie, right? But let's say you took a chance. You bought 100 Bitcoins for a few dollars. Fast forward to today, and those 100 Bitcoins are worth a fortune. We're talking millions of dollars!

Now, before you start daydreaming about buying a spaceship, listen up. Not every cryptocurrency is like Bitcoin, and not everyone who invested early became a millionaire. Some people did strike gold, but others found themselves holding worthless digital rocks. The point is, the possibility of making a lot of money is there, but so is the risk of losing a lot. Let's break it down a bit more.

The Roller Coaster Ride

If you've ever been on a roller coaster, you know how thrilling and nerve-wracking it can be. One moment you're climbing up, your heart pounding in anticipation. Then whoosh! Down you go at breakneck speed. Investing in cryptocurrencies can be similar. The price of a cryptocurrency can skyrocket but can also plummet. It's thrilling and terrifying at the same time.

The Word 'Volatility'

In the financial world, when prices go up and down dramatically, it's called "volatility." Cryptocurrencies are known for being highly volatile. This means you could invest $100 today and see it grow to $1,000 or even more. But, and this is a big BUT, it could also drop to

$10. Volatility is a double-edged sword. It gives you the chance to make high returns, but it also puts your investment at risk.

Supply and Demand

Ever wondered why prices change? It's a classic tale of supply and demand. If more people want a particular cryptocurrency, the price goes up. If people start selling it or lose interest, the price goes down. It's like a popular toy during the holidays. If every kid wants the same action figure, the price goes up because the toy is in high demand.

News and Hype

Now, what causes these changes in supply and demand? Often, it's news and hype. Let's say a famous billionaire tweets about a cryptocurrency. Suddenly, everyone wants to buy it, and the price goes up. But beware, the opposite can also happen. Bad news or rumors can cause prices to drop dramatically.

Regulation and Adoption

Imagine if a country decides to adopt a cryptocurrency as its official currency. That would make the price soar, right? But what if a country bans it? You guessed it, the price would most likely drop. Laws and regulations can play a significant role in how valuable a cryptocurrency becomes.

The Tech Behind It

Remember how we talked about blockchain technology? Sometimes, the promise of new or improved technology can drive up the price of a cryptocurrency. Investors often look for innovations that could make a cryptocurrency more useful or secure.

Diversification

If you've ever heard the saying, "Don't put all your eggs in one basket," then you know about diversification. It means spreading your investments across different types of assets. Many investors add cryptocurrencies to their portfolio as a form of diversification, hoping that if their other investments go down, the cryptocurrencies might go up.

Your Own Due Diligence

You can't rely on luck or gossip. If you're serious about investing in cryptocurrencies, you've got to do your homework. This is called "due diligence." It means researching and understanding what you're investing in. You wouldn't buy a car without checking if it works properly, right?

So, should you invest in cryptocurrencies for the potential high returns? That's a question only you can answer. Yes, people have made fortunes, but others have lost money too. It's a gamble, a risk, a roller coaster of a financial adventure.

In this digital treasure hunt, understanding the potential for high returns is your first clue. The rest is up to you, detective. Are you ready to continue unraveling the mystery? Because the journey is just as important as the destination, and you've got more ground to cover.

12.2 Diversification

Alright, adventurers, let's gather around for another chapter. If the last chapter was about the siren call of massive treasure, this one is about not getting sunk on the way. You see, even the most daring treasure hunters didn't put all their hopes into one chest of gold. No, they had maps to multiple treasures, just in case one turned out to be a dud or, even worse, a trap. In the world of investing, this strategy has a name: Diversification.

The All-Your-Eggs-in-One-Basket Problem

Imagine you have a basket, and in that basket, you put all your prized eggs—golden eggs, to be exact. You're pretty proud of these eggs, and they look stunning. But what if you trip and fall? Or what if someone steals your one and only basket? All your golden eggs are gone in a flash. That's the danger of putting all your resources in one place.

How Does Diversification Work?

In simple terms, diversification means spreading your investments around. It's like having multiple baskets for your eggs. If one basket falls, you've still got others safe and sound. In the realm of investing, instead of just having cryptocurrencies like Bitcoin or Ethereum, you might also invest in other things like stocks, bonds, or real estate.

The Financial Puzzle

Think of your investments as pieces of a giant puzzle. Each piece plays a role, and when put together, they make a complete picture. In this case, the picture is your financial stability and growth. By having different kinds of pieces—in this case, different kinds of investments—you are more likely to complete the puzzle successfully.

The Different Types of Baskets

So what are these different 'baskets' you could consider?

Stocks: These are shares of companies. You own a small part of the company and can benefit when they do well.

Bonds: These are like IOUs. You lend money to a company or the government, and they promise to pay you back with interest.

Real Estate: Buying property can be another way to grow your wealth over time.

Commodities: These are physical goods like gold, oil, or agricultural products.

Cryptocurrencies: Ah, yes, our main focus. Digital currencies that aren't controlled by any government.

Why Diversify in Cryptocurrencies?

Let's bring it back to crypto. Even within the world of cryptocurrencies, diversification is crucial. There are thousands of different cryptocurrencies out there. Some are established and stable (as stable as cryptocurrencies can be), like Bitcoin and Ethereum. Others are new and highly volatile, which means they could either soar to the sky or crash and burn.

By spreading your investments across multiple cryptocurrencies, you can protect yourself a bit better against the wild roller coaster of price changes.

Risks Everywhere

In the world of treasure hunting, there are all kinds of risks: booby traps, pirates, you name it. In investing, the risks might not be as thrilling but are equally real. Each type of investment comes with its own set of dangers. Stocks can crash. Real estate markets can slump. And, as you already know, cryptocurrencies can be super volatile. By diversifying, you reduce the impact these risks can have on your treasure chest.

Keeping an Eye on Your Baskets

Here's the thing: You can't just set it and forget it. Your investments need attention. Markets change, and new opportunities arise. Keeping track of your diversified portfolio requires time and, often, a well-thought-out strategy.

Timing and Research

The best treasure hunters always knew when to dig. Likewise, knowing when to invest in what is a skill that comes from lots of research and a good understanding of market trends. You'll need to keep an eye on news, understand global events that could affect your investments, and sometimes even consult experts.

Taxes and Fees

Oh, and diversification isn't free. Each investment can come with its own set of fees. Buying real estate? There are transaction costs. Investing in stocks? You might have to pay brokerage fees. Plus, remember that the taxman cometh, and each type of investment has its own tax rules.

The Balancing Act

Diversification is like walking a tightrope. You need to balance your investments to suit your needs, your financial goals, and your tolerance for risk. Some people might be okay with a portfolio that's a bit riskier if the potential for high returns is there. Others might prefer to play it safe, with more stable but less rewarding investments.

The Final Word

So, diversification isn't just a strategy; it's an ongoing process, an evolving plan. It's your safety net and your treasure map, all rolled into one. In the volatile world of cryptocurrencies, it can be the compass that guides you through turbulent waters. Choose your baskets wisely, keep an eye on them, and may your treasure hunting be ever prosperous.

So, are you ready to diversify? Choose wisely. Your financial future could depend on it.

12.3 Financial Sovereignty

Okay, team, let's navigate another chapter on our investing journey. So far, we've talked about making heaps of money and spreading our investments around like a treasure map. But there's another reason people are so hooked on cryptocurrencies. It's called "Financial Sovereignty." Big words, I know. Let's break it down.

The Big Words

So what does Financial Sovereignty even mean? Well, 'financial' is all about money, right? And 'sovereignty' is about being your own boss. Put them together, and you get the idea: Financial Sovereignty is about being in total control of your own money.

The Old Way

Let's rewind a bit. In the old days, and by old days I mean before cryptocurrencies, most people stored their money in banks. Seems safe, right? Banks have vaults, guards, and all that jazz. But here's the twist. Once your money is in the bank, you're not fully in control of it anymore. The bank is. Sure, they owe it to you, but they're the ones holding the keys to the vault.

The Problem With Third Parties

Why might that be a problem? Well, banks can make mistakes. They can even close down. Or imagine you're living in a country where the government isn't too trustworthy. They could freeze your account for no good reason. And then there's the whole thing about fees for every little transaction you make. Annoying, isn't it?

Enter Cryptocurrencies

This is where cryptocurrencies, like Bitcoin and Ethereum, come into the spotlight. With cryptocurrencies, there's no need for a bank. You become your own bank. Your money is stored in a digital wallet that only you can access. You hold the "keys" to your own financial kingdom. It's like having a treasure chest that only you can open, and you can carry it around with you wherever you go.

The Blockchain

The backbone of this system is something called a "blockchain." Think of it as an unbreakable digital chain that keeps your money safe. The blockchain is like a public record that everyone can see, but only you can access your part of it. That means there's no way for anyone to mess with your money.

Total Control

With cryptocurrencies, you have the final say on what happens to your money. Want to send some digital coins to a friend across the world? Go ahead. There's no bank to tell you, "Sorry, we're closed," or "That'll be a $25 fee, please." It's financial freedom in its purest form.

The Sword's Double-Edge

But hey, great power comes with great responsibility. When you're the boss of your own money, you've got no one to blame but yourself if something goes wrong. Lose the password to your digital wallet, and it's like dropping your treasure chest into the deepest part of the ocean. Gone for good.

Staying Safe

Financial Sovereignty sounds awesome, but it's not for the careless or the reckless. You have to be like a vigilant knight guarding their castle. That means keeping your digital keys safe, maybe even writing them down on paper and storing them in an actual safe. And always, always make sure you're not falling for scams or tricksters out there who'd love to plunder your treasure.

The Rules and Regulations

Being your own bank sounds like the Wild West, and in some ways, it is. But remember, even in the Wild West, there were sheriffs and laws. In the world of cryptocurrencies, rules are still being written. Governments are figuring out how to regulate digital money, how to tax it, and how to keep everyone playing fair.

For the Brave

Financial Sovereignty is for those brave enough to take full control of their financial future. It's not a journey for everyone. Some people are just more comfortable letting banks take care of their money, and that's totally fine. But for those who want to break free, to be the masters of their own financial destiny, cryptocurrencies offer a path.

The Future

We're at a turning point in history, my friends. Just like the printing press changed how we share information, cryptocurrencies could change how we think about money. Being in control of your own finances, without any middlemen, could be the new normal one day.

Your Mission

So here's your mission, should you choose to accept it. Ask yourself: Are you ready for the responsibility of being your own bank? Can you handle the power and the risk that come with Financial Sovereignty? If the answer is yes, then welcome to a brave new world. Your financial future is in your hands, literally.

The Final Word

Financial Sovereignty isn't just a fad or a buzzword; it's a paradigm shift, a new way of seeing the world. If you opt in, you're part of a revolution—a revolution where you're the hero, fighting for your own financial freedom. But remember, every hero needs to be well-prepared, well-armed, and well-aware of the challenges that lie ahead.

And so, our chapter on Financial Sovereignty comes to a close. Like any good adventure, it's filled with promise, risks, and a treasure chest that only you hold the key to. Choose wisely. Your financial future is, quite literally, in your own hands.

12.4 Key Takeaways

Alright, folks, time to recap what we've learned in this hefty chapter on why investing in cryptocurrencies might just be the adventure you've been waiting for. Grab your compass; here are the coordinates for your treasure map.

1. Potential for High Returns

Cryptocurrencies can offer sky-high profits, but remember, there's a flip side—risks are high too. It's like a roller coaster, thrilling but can also be stomach-churning. Do your homework before you jump on the ride.

2. Diversification

In the world of investments, putting all your eggs in one basket is never a good idea. Cryptocurrencies offer you a way to add some variety to your treasure chest. But make sure you understand the other investments you're mixing in there.

3. Financial Sovereignty

Being your own bank is empowering but also comes with a heap of responsibilities. You're the guardian of your own treasure, so make sure you've got your armor on and your sword sharpened (figuratively, of course).

4. Rules and Regulations

Even in the Wild West of cryptocurrencies, laws are starting to take shape. Being aware of these rules is like knowing the lay of the land—you'll be better prepared to navigate the challenges and avoid stepping into quicksand.

5. Risks

The risks in cryptocurrency are as real as they come. It's like sailing in uncharted waters; you never know when a storm might hit. Always be prepared and make sure you've got your lifejacket on—that's your research and risk management strategies.

6. Future is Uncertain but Exciting

We're at the frontier of a new world in finance. It's like being the first explorers on a new continent. The landscape is still being mapped out, and nobody knows for sure what we'll find. But for those with the spirit of adventure, it's an irresistible call.

7. Your Mission

If you decide that this cryptocurrency journey is for you, remember you're taking the reins of your own financial future. Be bold, but be wise. Every hero has to plan before going on their quest.

And there you have it. The key takeaways from our chapter on why to invest in cryptocurrencies. This isn't just another page in your financial story; it could very well be the start of a brand new chapter. But like any story worth telling, it's got its heroes and villains, its treasures and traps.

Choose your path wisely, adventurers. The next chapter is yours to write.

Crypto Simplified: A Beginner's Guide to Understanding Bitcoin, Blockchain, and Cryptocurrency Investing - by Kenneth K. Lee

Section 13: Basic Investment Strategies

Alright, so you're fascinated by the world of cryptocurrencies, and you're considering diving into this digital treasure hunt. But let's not fool ourselves; finding gold isn't as simple as following a rainbow. If only it were, right? So, before you start loading up your digital wallet like a pirate's chest, you'll want some strategies—some plans—to make your quest a successful one. Welcome to the chapter where we take off the training wheels: Basic Investment Strategies.

Here's the thing. Imagine you're the captain of a ship. You wouldn't set sail without a map, would you? Investment strategies are like your navigational charts. They help you set a course, deal with storms, and hopefully, lead you to the treasure you're seeking.

First up, we'll talk about "Long-Term Holding." Now, don't be fooled by the simple name. This strategy is all about patience and grit, like a treasure hunter waiting years to decipher a riddle. You buy your digital gold—your cryptocurrencies—and hold onto them for a long period, even when the seas get rough. The idea is that the longer you hold, the more valuable your treasure might become.

Next, we move onto "Trading." If Long-Term Holding is like a patient treasure hunter, then Trading is more like a skilled swordfighter, always ready to act. In trading, timing is everything. Buy low, sell high, and do it all over again. It sounds easy, but let me tell you, it's as complex as any duel. You need to know when to strike and when to parry, and that takes skill.

Then there's "Diversification," a word as big as a pirate ship and just as important. Ever heard the saying, "Don't put all your eggs in one basket?" Well, don't put all your treasure in one chest. You'll want different types of cryptocurrencies, maybe even some non-crypto investments, to spread out the risk. Think of it like assembling a crew of pirates—each with their own skills to help you on your quest.

We'll also talk about "Risk Management." The seas are unpredictable, and so is the world of cryptocurrency. Risk management is like the experienced first mate who helps the captain make smarter decisions. It's about knowing what kind of risks you're okay with and how to reduce the ones you're not. And no, it's not as boring as it sounds. A smart pirate is a successful pirate.

And lastly, we'll look at "Technical and Fundamental Analysis." These are your spyglasses, the tools that help you scan the horizon for opportunities or dangers. These analyses are how you read the market's winds and tides, helping you make your investment decisions.

Now, I want you to remember something very important. In the world of cryptocurrencies, there are no guarantees. The market is as mysterious as the deepest ocean and just as full of surprises. You might find sunken treasure, or you might run into sea monsters. Your strategies are your safeguards, but like any adventure, the outcome is never certain.

So, grab your compass and your map, my friends. We're about to set sail into the challenging but thrilling waters of cryptocurrency investment strategies. It's time to plot a course for your financial future. Are you ready? Because your next adventure is about to begin.

13.1 HODLing

Welcome to the world of HODLing, a term that might sound like it belongs in a medieval castle with knights and wizards. But, no, HODLing is a strategy in the modern world of cryptocurrency. Imagine you're a treasure hunter who's found a precious gem. The gem's value could skyrocket in the future. So what do you do? You lock it in a chest, bury it, and guard it for years, hoping it'll turn into an even bigger fortune. That's essentially what HODLing is. You buy cryptocurrencies and keep them locked away in your digital treasure chest.

Let's start with the weird name, shall we? "HODL" stands for "Hold On for Dear Life." Yep, you read that right. The term comes from a misspelled word "hold," and it took a life of its own in the crypto community. It describes a strategy where you buy and hold onto a cryptocurrency, like Bitcoin, Ethereum, or any other digital coin, for a long time, even when the market is up and down like a ship in a stormy sea.

Now, why would someone choose to HODL? Well, history shows us that some of the most valuable things in life take time to grow. Think about it. The oak tree starts as an acorn. Rome wasn't built in a day. Good things, as they say, come to those who wait.

Remember the early days of Bitcoin? Some people bought the digital coin when it was worth less than a dollar. They held onto it, despite the critics and the skeptics, the booms and the busts. Fast forward to today, and one Bitcoin is worth a lot more. Those who HODLed are like pirates who discovered a sunken treasure.

But don't think HODLing is just for the risk-takers who dive into the unknown for buried treasure. It can be a strategy for the cautious as well. You see, the cryptocurrency market is like a wild ocean, full of high waves and deep troughs. Prices can shoot up one day and plummet the next. If you're the type of person who gets seasick with all these ups and downs, HODLing is like staying anchored in a safe harbor, waiting for the storm to pass.

However, even though HODLing sounds simple, it's not for the faint of heart. Imagine watching your treasure chest go from being worth a king's ransom to the price of a loaf of bread, all in a matter of weeks. That's happened in the crypto world, and it's not easy to hold on, let me tell you. It takes nerves of steel to HODL, especially when everyone else is screaming, "Sell! Sell! Sell!"

Before you decide to HODL, do your homework. Research the cryptocurrency you're interested in. Is it a solid coin with a strong future, or is it a "shiny object" that might lose its luster? The last thing you want is to HODL a worthless trinket.

You should also consider how long you're willing to keep your treasure buried. Some people HODL for a few years, while others plan to never sell. Make sure to think about your own goals and needs. Are you saving for something specific? Retirement, maybe? Or perhaps you just like the idea of owning a piece of the future. Either way, know what you're getting into.

To sum it up, HODLing is a long-term game. It's the strategy of buying and holding, through the good times and the bad, with the hope that your digital treasure will be worth more in the future. But remember, like any treasure hunt, there are no guarantees. You might find a chest full of gold, or you might end up with a box of rocks.

So, if you're planning to become a HODLer, make sure you've got the courage and the patience of a legendary treasure hunter. It's an adventure, after all, and every adventure comes with its share of risks and rewards. Are you ready to embark on this exciting journey?

13.2 Active Trading

Now, let's venture into another landscape of the crypto world: Active Trading. If HODLing is like being a patient treasure hunter, then active trading is like being a swashbuckling pirate, navigating through turbulent waters, sword in hand, eyes always on the lookout for the next big opportunity. Both can be thrilling, but active trading demands your constant attention, like a high-speed chase across the seven seas.

Imagine you're the captain of a pirate ship. You've got a map, but instead of X marks the spot, you've got constantly changing numbers, graphs, and charts. Your treasure? Well, it's not buried in some remote island; it's floating in the open sea, waiting for you to seize it. But be warned, fellow pirate; the sea is filled with other captains, and they're all after the same treasure.

What is active trading? Simply put, it's buying and selling cryptocurrencies in a short period, sometimes even within seconds. The goal is to take advantage of small price changes to make a profit. It's like buying a barrel of rum at one island and selling it at the next for a higher price. You have to be quick, smart, and a little bit daring.

In active trading, time is of the essence. Every second count. Just like a pirate needs a good telescope to spot distant ships or lands, an active trader needs good tools. These include real-time price charts, technical analysis software, and a reliable internet connection. Without these, you'd be like a ship without a compass—lost and directionless.

So how do you get started? First, you choose a trading platform, like a pirate chooses a ship. Make sure it's reliable and has all the tools you need. Next, you deposit some cryptocurrency into your account, just like how a ship needs to be loaded with cannons and supplies before it sets sail.

Once you're ready, it's time to start trading. But here's where it gets tricky. The crypto market is volatile; prices can soar high into the sky or dive deep into the ocean in a blink of an eye. That's why active trading is not for everyone. It requires a good understanding of the market trends and a lot of practice. It's like learning how to navigate through dangerous waters; one wrong move and you might sink your ship.

There are different types of active trading strategies, like "day trading," where you buy and sell on short-term movements within the market. Another one is "swing trading," where you take advantage of price "swings" in the market. Then there's "scalping," where you try to make small profits from short-term price changes. Each has its own risks and rewards, like different pirate paths to treasure.

Speaking of risks, let's talk about the darker side of active trading. Just as a pirate faces the dangers of storms, sea monsters, and other pirates, an active trader faces risks too. You could make wrong predictions, and lose money. You could be so caught up in the excitement that you make reckless decisions. Or, the market could change suddenly due to unforeseen events, like a powerful nation declaring war against pirates or a sudden collapse in the value of a currency.

That's why it's essential to have a solid strategy. Some traders even set up "stop-loss" orders, which automatically sell their cryptocurrencies if the price falls to a certain level, minimizing losses. Think of it as an emergency escape plan when you're cornered by an enemy ship.

And let's not forget about the costs. Active trading involves frequent buying and selling, which means you'll have to pay fees, like a pirate docking at multiple ports. Over time, these fees can add up and eat into your profits.

Despite the risks and costs, many find active trading thrilling. Every day is a new adventure with challenges to overcome and treasures to find. But, you have to be prepared, both mentally and emotionally. Make sure to practice, maybe start with a smaller amount of money that you can afford to lose. Test out your strategies, learn from your mistakes, and always be on the lookout for new opportunities. The market never sleeps, and neither do the most successful pirates.

To sum it up, active trading is a fast-paced, high-risk, and potentially high-reward strategy in the cryptocurrency world. It's for those who seek thrills and are willing to put in the time and effort to navigate the choppy waters. But remember, being a swashbuckling pirate of the crypto sea is not for everyone. So, weigh the risks carefully and decide if this is the adventure you wish to embark on.

And there you have it, young crypto adventurers. We've sailed through the intriguing world of active trading. Whether you choose to be a patient treasure hunter or a daring pirate is entirely up to you. But whichever path you choose, make sure you're well-equipped for the journey ahead. Ahoy!

13.3 Dollar-Cost Averaging

Alright, explorers of the cryptocurrency frontier, we've talked about HODLing—where you buy and hold onto your crypto like it's a treasured artifact. We've also discussed active trading—the daring escapade of buying and selling in quick succession, like a swashbuckling pirate on high seas. Now, let's talk about another strategy, one that's more like being a wise old traveler who takes each step cautiously but steadily. This strategy is called Dollar-Cost Averaging, or DCA for short.

Imagine you're on a journey to find a hidden treasure, but instead of rushing ahead or waiting for the perfect moment, you decide to take your time. You move forward step by step, collecting small treasures along the way. You're not worried about whether today is the best day to find treasure; you're focused on the long game.

Dollar-Cost Averaging is sort of like that. In this strategy, you invest a fixed amount of money in cryptocurrency at regular intervals—be it weekly, bi-weekly, or monthly—regardless of its price. It's like going to the market every Saturday to buy apples. Sometimes the apples are expensive, sometimes they're cheap, but you always buy the same amount of money's worth.

Why would you do that, you ask? Good question. You see, the price of cryptocurrencies can be as unpredictable as the weather. One moment it's sunny and pleasant; the next, a storm rolls in out of nowhere. If you try to time the market perfectly, buying low and selling high, you might end up caught in the rain more often than you'd like.

But with DCA, you don't have to worry about timing the market just right. You invest the same amount of money each time, no matter what. When prices are high, you end up buying less of the cryptocurrency, like getting fewer apples when they're expensive. But when prices are low, your fixed amount of money buys you more, like a bigger bag of apples for the same price.

Over time, this approach averages out the cost of your investment. That's why it's called Dollar-Cost Averaging. You may not hit the jackpot instantly, but you're also less likely to suffer great losses. It's a cautious yet consistent way to grow your investment, like a gardener patiently watering a plant, come rain or shine.

Let's say you're investing in a cryptocurrency called 'CryptoGold.' You decide to invest $50 every week. The first week, the price is high, so you get less CryptoGold for your $50. The next week, the price dips, and your $50 buys you more. Over several weeks and months, the highs and lows average out. In the end, you have a sizable amount of CryptoGold that you bought at an average price. You didn't get the best deal ever, but you also avoided the worst. It's about consistency, not timing.

Now, just like every strategy, DCA has its pros and cons. The upside is that it's straightforward and low-stress. You don't have to be a market wizard, glued to price charts and news updates. You set a plan, stick to it, and let time do its work. The downside? Well, because you're investing over time, you might miss out on opportunities to buy at rock-bottom prices. But remember, DCA is not about getting rich quick; it's about building wealth steadily.

Some folks might say that DCA is boring, like a long hike through a familiar forest. There aren't many surprises, and you're not hunting for quick wins. But don't underestimate the power of steady progress. Just like a river shapes a mountain over eons, Dollar-Cost Averaging can shape your financial future over years.

It's also worth mentioning that while DCA is a safer strategy, it's not completely risk-free. The cryptocurrency market is still a wild frontier, and anything can happen. That's why it's crucial to only invest money you can afford to lose. Think of it as packing only what you can carry on a long journey—overloading yourself can slow you down or even make you trip.

Before you start, you'll need to choose which cryptocurrency you want to invest in, how much you want to invest, and how often. Once that's decided, you set up automatic payments, so you don't even have to think about it. It's like setting a calendar reminder for your journey—every week or month, you'll know it's time to move a step closer to your goal.

So, there you have it. Dollar-Cost Averaging: the slow and steady strategy for the patient traveler in the volatile world of cryptocurrencies. It may not have the excitement of active trading or the allure of striking gold with a one-time investment, but it's got its own kind of wisdom: the wisdom of consistency.

And remember, in the world of investment, as in life, there's more than one path to treasure. The important thing is to choose the one that suits you best. Whether you're a HODLer, an active trader, or a dollar-cost averager, the journey is all yours. So prepare well, be patient, and keep moving forward. Safe travels, fellow explorers.

13.4 Key Takeaways

Alright, let's recap what we've discovered on this section of our journey through the land of cryptocurrency investment strategies.

1. **HODLing:** This is the treasure-hunter approach. You buy your crypto and hang onto it for dear life, hoping it will increase in value over time. It's simple, but it also means you have to be patient and weather the storms.
2. **Active Trading:** This is for the adventurers who like the thrill of the chase. You're constantly buying and selling, trying to make profits in the short term. It's exciting but requires a lot of time, attention, and skill.
3. **Dollar-Cost Averaging (DCA):** Think of this as the steady traveler's path. You invest a fixed amount of money at regular intervals, regardless of whether the crypto market is up or down. Over time, this can average out the price you pay for your investment.

Each strategy has its pros and cons:

- **HODLing** is simple and requires less effort, but you have to deal with market ups and downs.
- **Active Trading** can offer quick profits, but it's risky and time-consuming.
- **DCA** is a more cautious approach that allows for steady investment, but you may miss out on the lowest prices.

And let's not forget, no matter which path you choose, there are risks involved. The cryptocurrency market is still like a wild frontier, where unexpected things can happen anytime. So always be prepared and only invest what you can afford to lose.

Remember, there's no one-size-fits-all strategy in the world of cryptocurrencies. Your journey is yours alone, and the strategy you pick should suit your goals, lifestyle, and risk tolerance.

So, take what you've learned, pick your path, and continue your adventure in the cryptocurrency landscape. Each strategy is like a different trail in a vast forest—some are easy walks, some are challenging climbs, but all of them lead to new discoveries.

Happy exploring, everyone!

Section 14: How to Analyze a Cryptocurrency

You've ever heard the phrase "don't judge a book by its cover," right? Well, the same could be said about cryptocurrencies. At first glance, they might all look the same—a digital form of money. But each one is a different chapter in the grand story of the financial revolution. And just like with books, if you don't look closely, you might miss out on an epic tale or get stuck in a storyline that goes nowhere.

So, how do you separate the heroes from the villains in the world of cryptocurrencies? That's what this section is all about. Think of it as your detective's handbook, your guide to unraveling the mysteries that lie within the world of digital coins. We're going to put on our detective hats and look for clues that will tell us whether a cryptocurrency is worth investing in or best left on the shelf.

We'll explore topics like market cap, which is a bit like judging the popularity of a book. If everyone's reading it, there might be something special about it, right? We'll also get into things like liquidity. Imagine you found a rare gem of a book that nobody knows about. It might be valuable, but if no one's interested, you can't really sell it, can you? That's liquidity in a nutshell.

Technology plays a huge part too. In the world of books, it might be the quality of writing and the depth of research. In the world of crypto, it's the coding and the security features. Is this coin's technology innovative, or is it a copycat? Does it offer something that could change the world, or is it just full of empty promises?

And then there's the community. In the world of books, a strong fan base can make a book a bestseller. In crypto, a strong community can do wonders too. They can help with development, spread the word, and even defend the coin against critics. But, as we'll learn, not all communities are created equal.

We'll also talk about the people who make the coins—the developers and the founders. Are they credible? Do they have a track record of success? Or are they mysterious figures with no past? It's a lot like knowing if a book is written by a Pulitzer Prize-winning author or someone who has never written a sentence before.

While we're at it, we'll also dig into regulatory issues. Laws and rules might sound boring, but trust me, they're crucial. Imagine if a book was banned in several countries. That would raise some red flags, right? Same goes for cryptocurrencies. We'll learn about what makes a cryptocurrency more or less risky in the eyes of the law.

We'll finish up by pulling all these clues together to make an informed decision. Think of it as writing your own review of the cryptocurrency. You'll learn to look at all the angles, weigh the pros and cons, and make a judgment based on solid evidence.

So, are you ready to become a cryptocurrency detective? Good. Put on your trench coat, grab your magnifying glass, and let's dive in. It's time to unravel the secrets and mysteries of cryptocurrencies, one clue at a time. Because in this fast-paced world of digital money, being a good detective can make all the difference between choosing the next big thing and falling for a scam.

Let's start cracking some cases.

14.1 Market Cap

Alright, detective, your first clue in analyzing a cryptocurrency is something called "Market Cap." Sounds fancy, right? But don't worry, it's not as complicated as it sounds. Market Cap is short for Market Capitalization, and it's a number that tells us how big a particular cryptocurrency is in the grand scheme of things.

Picture this: you're at a school fair, and there are different booths selling stuff. Some booths are drawing huge crowds, and some are kind of lonely. You'd naturally think the crowded booths are more popular, right? And if you had to guess, you'd say they're probably making more money. Market Cap is a similar idea. It gives you a quick idea of how popular and valuable a cryptocurrency is compared to others.

Here's the math part, but don't panic. To find the Market Cap, you multiply the current price of one coin by the total number of coins that exist. For example, if each coin costs $10 and there are 1 million coins, the Market Cap would be $10 million. Simple, right?

Now you're probably wondering why this number is so important. Well, a high Market Cap usually means a lot of people are investing in that coin. It's like a book that everyone is reading; there's probably something special about it. But remember, just because a book is popular doesn't always mean it's good. Same goes for cryptocurrencies. A high Market Cap might grab your attention, but it shouldn't be the only thing you look at.

On the flip side, a low Market Cap isn't always bad news. Think about that booth at the fair that's a little lonely. Maybe they're selling something brand new that people haven't discovered yet. Or maybe they're selling something so unique that only a few people are interested. Cryptocurrencies with low Market Caps can be like hidden treasures. But be careful, they can also be riskier.

You see, with a high Market Cap, a cryptocurrency is more stable. It's like a big ship in the ocean; it takes a lot to make it sink. But a low Market Cap is like a small boat; a big wave can tip it over easily. In other words, low Market Cap coins can be more volatile. The price can shoot up really fast, but it can also drop just as quickly.

But wait, there's more. Market Cap can also tell us something about a coin's potential for growth. Imagine a small booth at the fair suddenly getting lots of attention because they started selling something amazing. They could become the next big thing! The same could happen to a low Market Cap coin. If it has a solid plan and a good team behind it, its Market Cap could skyrocket.

On the other hand, a coin with an already high Market Cap might not have as much room to grow. It's like a best-selling book that everyone's already read. Chances are, its days of skyrocketing sales are over.

Alright, time for some real talk. Market Cap is just one clue in our detective toolkit. It's a great starting point, but don't stop there. Would you decide if a book is good based only on how many people are reading it? Probably not. You'd look at reviews, maybe read a sample, and check out who the author is. In the same way, Market Cap should be your first stop in analyzing a cryptocurrency, not your last.

So, to sum it up, Market Cap can tell you:

1. How popular and valuable a cryptocurrency is.
2. How stable or risky it might be.
3. Its potential for growth.

Put on your detective glasses, jot these notes down in your detective notebook, and let's move on to the next clue. Remember, a good detective never relies on just one piece of evidence. And in the world of cryptocurrency, the more clues you have, the closer you'll get to solving the mystery.

Ready for the next clue? Let's dive deeper into the world of cryptocurrency and unlock more secrets. Because in this digital treasure hunt, every clue counts.

14.2 Volume

Okay, young investigators, you've already cracked the code on Market Cap, but that was just the opening act. Our next clue in this digital mystery is called "Volume." Now, before you start thinking about the volume on your TV or music player, let's get one thing straight—this is a different kind of volume. And just like Market Cap, it's a big clue in figuring out what's going on with a cryptocurrency.

Imagine you're standing next to a busy freeway. Cars are whizzing by so fast you can barely count them. That road has high volume. Now, picture a quiet country lane where just a few cars pass by every hour. That's low volume. In the world of cryptocurrencies, volume is all about how much of a specific coin is being traded in a given period—usually a day.

"Why should I care?" you might ask. Excellent question. Volume tells us about interest and activity. If a coin has high trading volume, it's like that busy freeway: lots of people are interested and there's a lot happening. This usually means something's up—maybe good news about the coin, maybe bad news. But either way, people are paying attention.

Let's say you hear about a hot new video game that everyone's talking about. If you walk into a store and see that game flying off the shelves, you know the buzz is real. High volume in cryptocurrency is similar. When a lot of people are buying and selling, it usually means something significant is happening, and you might want to pay attention too.

However, just like traffic jams aren't always a good thing, high volume isn't always positive. It could mean people are buying up a coin because they're excited about it, which could drive the price up. Or, it could mean everyone's trying to sell their coins, maybe because there's bad news, which could drive the price down. High volume, like a noisy room, is full of energy—but it's up to you to figure out if that energy is good or bad.

Now, let's flip the coin. What about low volume? Well, if a cryptocurrency has low trading volume, it's like that quiet country lane—peaceful, sure, but maybe a little too quiet. In crypto terms, low volume usually means not many people are trading the coin. Maybe they don't know about it, or maybe they just don't care.

So, is low volume bad? Not necessarily. Remember our lonely booth at the fair from our Market Cap discussion? Low volume might mean the coin is like a hidden gem waiting to be discovered. But, and it's a big but, low volume can also mean higher risk. Think about walking on thin ice—the less support you have, the riskier it is.

Alright, here's something else to ponder. Volume can be like a magnifying glass for Market Cap. Say you find a coin with a high Market Cap but low volume. That could be a red flag. Why? Because it might mean that even though the coin looks big and popular, not much is actually happening with it. On the other hand, a high Market Cap and high volume? Now, that's a coin that not only has a crowd but also has the crowd's attention.

Before we wrap up, let's throw in a detective tip: Watch for sudden changes in volume. If a usually quiet coin suddenly has a spike in volume, it's like a quiet person shouting. Something's up, and it's time to dig deeper.

So, what have we learned, detectives?

1. Volume shows us how much interest and activity there is around a coin.
2. High volume could mean something big is happening, but you have to figure out if it's good or bad.
3. Low volume isn't necessarily bad, but it usually means higher risk.
4. Volume can magnify what we learn from Market Cap, helping us see the full picture.

Jot these down in your detective notebook. With Market Cap and Volume in your toolkit, you're well on your way to becoming a cryptocurrency whiz. But don't close the case just yet. We've got more clues to find, more puzzles to solve, and more secrets to uncover.

Ready for your next assignment? Keep those detective hats on, because the next clue might just crack this case wide open. Onward!

14.3 Price Charts

Ah, Price Charts—the maps to the treasure, the X-rays of the crypto world, the graphs that look like roller coasters for numbers. If you think maps are just for pirates or that X-rays are only for superheroes, you've got another thing coming. In the complex landscape of cryptocurrency, a Price Chart is as crucial as a compass is to a sailor.

Imagine this: You're an explorer in a dense jungle. The trees are tall, and the path is windy and confusing. You have a map sketched by someone who went before you. It shows the dangerous cliffs to avoid, the rivers you'll have to cross, and maybe, just maybe, the spot where treasure is buried. A Price Chart is sort of like that map. It helps you navigate the ups and downs, the risks and rewards of the cryptocurrency world.

Let's break it down. A Price Chart generally shows how the price of a particular cryptocurrency has changed over time. Most Price Charts have two axes. The horizontal axis, or the one that runs from left to right, represents time. This could be as short as a single day or as long as several years. The vertical axis, or the one that goes up and down, shows the price.

"Big deal," you might say. "It's just a line going up and down." Well, not so fast, junior detective. That line tells a story—a story of battles won and lost, of fortunes made and squandered. In short, each point on that line can be a clue. It could point you to why a cryptocurrency skyrocketed in value or plummeted to the depths.

But wait, there's more! Charts come in different flavors. You might have heard of line charts, bar charts, and the more exotic-sounding candlestick charts. Each type of chart gives you different insights.

1. **Line Charts** - These are your basic charts. A line connects the closing prices of a cryptocurrency over a specific period. Simple, but sometimes simplicity is genius.
2. **Bar Charts** - A bit more complicated. Each bar shows the opening and closing prices and also the highest and lowest points the cryptocurrency reached. It's like seeing the whole battlefield, not just the final score.
3. **Candlestick Charts** - Now, we're getting into the expert level. These charts not only show the opening, closing, high, and low prices, but they also give a sense of market sentiment. Green candles generally mean prices went up. Red candles mean they went down. It's like reading the mood of the room without even walking in.

Now you may wonder, "How do I read these charts?" Excellent question. Reading a Price Chart is similar to reading music or maybe even Morse code. At first, it looks confusing, a bunch of lines or dots or squiggles. But as you get the hang of it, you start seeing patterns. You notice that before a price goes up, it often does a certain little dance—a zig here, a zag there. These patterns have names like "Head and Shoulders," "Double Bottom," and "Cup and Handle."

And why should you care about these patterns? Because, dear investigator, patterns often repeat themselves. Spotting a pattern can be like seeing storm clouds on the horizon. You can prepare for rain. Or in crypto terms, you might get clues about whether a price will go up or down.

But beware—the map is not the territory. Price Charts show what has happened, not what will happen. They're valuable, but they're not fortune-telling crystal balls. Like a weather forecast, they give you an idea, a suggestion, a hint. The storm might change course. The treasure might be a myth.

So, in summary, what's in our detective notebook?

1. Price Charts are like maps, guiding you through the ups and downs of cryptocurrency prices.
2. Different types of charts give you different kinds of information. Choose your chart like you choose your tool in a treasure hunt.
3. Reading a Price Chart is an acquired skill. The better you get at spotting patterns, the better you'll be at anticipating price movements.
4. Charts show the past, not the future. They're valuable guides but not guarantees.

There you go, crypto cadets. You're now equipped with another tool in your investigative kit. So, put on your detective cap, roll out those

Price Charts, and let's dig deeper. The clues are out there, and they're waiting for you to find them. Onward to the next chapter in this crypto saga!

14.4 Key Takeaways

Alright, let's put on the brakes for a moment and take stock of what we've learned in this section. Think of this as your treasure map's legend, the part that tells you what all those squiggly lines and symbols actually mean. Here's the rundown:

1. **Understanding Price Charts is Critical:** Just like a treasure map helps you navigate through unknown terrain, Price Charts guide you through the labyrinth of cryptocurrency investments.
2. **Types of Charts:** We have line charts, bar charts, and candlestick charts. Line charts are the simplest, giving you just the basics. Bar charts go a step further, revealing highs and lows. Candlestick charts, the most advanced of the bunch, give you a sense of the market's mood—whether it's a bull party or a bear's lair.
3. **Reading is a Skill:** Like reading sheet music or Morse code, interpreting a Price Chart is a skill you get better at over time. It involves recognizing patterns, each with its own fancy name like "Head and Shoulders" or "Double Bottom," which can give you clues on what might happen next.
4. **Patterns Repeat, But No Guarantees:** As much as we love a good pattern, remember it's a guide, not a guarantee. Charts are excellent at telling us what happened in the past, but they're not crystal balls that predict the future. Proceed with caution.
5. **Charts Aren't Everything:** While Price Charts are incredibly useful, they're just one tool in your toolkit. They give you a

snapshot of past behavior, but remember, the past is not always a perfect predictor of the future.
6. **Understand the Limits:** Price Charts provide insights, but they also have their limitations. They show historical data and can indicate trends, but external factors like news events can change the game entirely.

So there it is—your quick guide to the key points of Price Charts. Keep this list handy, because understanding how to analyze a cryptocurrency isn't just about the numbers; it's about understanding the stories those numbers tell. And who knows? With the right set of tools, you might just become the Sherlock Holmes of the crypto world.

Onward, crypto detectives! The next chapter awaits, and it promises to be just as thrilling as this one.

Section 15: Understanding Risks and Volatility

Let's set the scene. Imagine you're the captain of a ship sailing on the high seas. The sun is shining, and the wind fills your sails as you glide effortlessly through the water. It's almost like the world is tipping its hat to you, rewarding your bravery and skill. But wait—just when you start getting comfortable, storm clouds roll in, and the waters grow rough. Now you're in for a real test of your abilities.

In the world of cryptocurrency, it's a bit like that. One moment you're riding high on a wave of success, and the next, you're navigating through a storm of uncertainty. Just as sailors need to be aware of weather patterns and other risks on their voyages, crypto investors need to understand the risks and volatility that come with investing in digital currencies. It's not just about basking in the sunny days; it's about being prepared for the storms that inevitably come.

Now, 'volatility' might sound like a word that belongs in a science textbook, but trust me, it's pretty straightforward. It basically means how much the price of something, like a cryptocurrency, goes up and down over a certain period. Think of it as the ocean's waves: sometimes calm and predictable, sometimes wild and unruly.

And then there's 'risk.' Ah, risk—the word that makes many people's palms sweaty. In our ship metaphor, risks are the rocks, pirates, and storms that could wreck your journey. In crypto, risks are things like scams, changes in laws, or the entire market taking a nosedive.

Why is it important to understand these terms? Well, they're like the compass and barometer on your ship. They help you make decisions based on more than just a hunch or a hopeful glance at the sky. You see, every investment has some level of risk, just like every sea voyage has its dangers. But by understanding the nature of these risks and how to navigate through them, you arm yourself with the tools to make smarter choices.

In this section, we're going to dig deep into what makes the crypto market so, let's say, 'exciting.' We'll look at the various factors that contribute to its volatility. Is it market sentiment? Is it news and events? Or is it the ever-changing regulations that govern this digital frontier?

We'll also explore the kinds of risks you'll encounter on your crypto journey. We're talking about market risks, regulatory risks, and even the risk of getting hacked. Trust me, these are not tales from a horror book but very real scenarios that you need to be prepared for.

Don't worry; it's not all doom and gloom. For every risk, there's a strategy to mitigate it. For every turbulent wave, there's a way to steer the ship safely. This section aims to arm you with the knowledge to do just that.

So, put on your captain's hat and grab your telescope. The waters of cryptocurrency investing are choppy, and it's easy to get lost or shipwrecked. But with the right understanding of risks and volatility, you can navigate through them like a seasoned sailor, ready to face whatever comes your way.

Ready? Steady. Sail on. The next chapter is waiting for you, and it's one you won't want to skip.

15.1 Market Volatility

Alright, let's get straight to it. Market volatility is like the weather of the cryptocurrency world. You know how the weather can change quickly? One minute it's sunny, and the next, you're caught in a downpour? Well, the price of cryptocurrencies can behave the same way. It's as if Mother Nature herself is controlling the crypto market, making it sunny one moment and stormy the next.

Now, you might wonder, why is the crypto market so jittery? Great question. There are many reasons, and they're kind of like the ingredients in a recipe. Each one adds a different flavor, and together, they create the taste of the market. Let's break it down.

News and Events

First up, news and events. Imagine you're sailing your ship, and you see dark clouds forming in the distance. You know a storm is coming, so you get ready. In the crypto market, a big news story can be that dark cloud. Maybe a country decides to ban cryptocurrencies, or perhaps a major company starts accepting Bitcoin. News like this can send ripples through the market, making prices shoot up or tumble down.

Market Sentiment

Then we have market sentiment, which is basically how people are feeling about cryptocurrencies. Are they optimistic? Pessimistic? This sentiment is like the wind for your sail. A positive vibe can make your crypto journey smooth, but a negative one can make it choppy. It's as if the emotions of all the traders got bottled up and poured into the market, causing it to rise and fall like the tide.

Supply and Demand

Don't forget about supply and demand, the age-old duo. Imagine a bunch of ships all heading to the same treasure island. If only a few ships know about it, there's enough treasure for everyone. But if everyone's rushing there, suddenly that treasure becomes a hot commodity, and its value rises. The same thing happens in crypto.

When many people want a particular coin but there's only a limited supply, the price goes up.

Regulation Changes

Last but not least, let's talk about regulations, or the "rules of the sea." Just as maritime laws govern how ships operate, regulations control how cryptocurrencies work. When a government sets new rules or changes old ones, it can make waves in the crypto world. Investors get nervous or excited, and the market reacts accordingly.

Now, volatility isn't all bad. For some traders, it's like a game of strategy. When prices go down, it's an opportunity to buy low. When prices go up, it's a chance to sell high. But remember, it's a game that comes with high stakes. One wrong move, and you might find yourself in troubled waters.

So, how can you navigate through this choppy sea of market volatility? Well, there are tools and strategies for that, like doing your own research and not putting all your eggs—or in this case, coins—in one basket. And just like how sailors use maps and compasses, traders use charts and data to predict market trends.

In a nutshell, market volatility is part and parcel of the crypto universe. It's like the weather—you can't control it, but you can certainly prepare for it. By understanding the factors that cause these price swings, you become a better sailor in the tumultuous seas of cryptocurrency.

So, put on your raincoat and ready your lifejacket. You're not just along for the ride; you're the captain of your own ship. And like any good captain, you need to be prepared for whatever the sea—or in this case, the market—throws your way.

15.2 Regulatory Risks

Ah, regulations. That word might sound boring, but trust me, it's anything but. Regulations are the rules of the road in the world of money, and when it comes to cryptocurrencies, they're like the ever-changing map of a treasure hunt. One wrong turn, and you could find yourself lost or, worse, in a heap of trouble. Let's dig deeper into what these regulatory risks are and why they matter.

The Law of the Land

First off, it's good to know that laws are not the same everywhere. Just like different countries have different rules for driving, they also have different rules for cryptocurrencies. One country might welcome crypto with open arms, while another might treat it like a pirate treats a naval officer — not well, to say the least.

In some places, governments have banned cryptocurrencies entirely. Think of it as being told that you can't even hunt for treasure in those parts of the ocean. In other places, you might be able to own and use cryptocurrencies, but with a lot of strings attached. For instance, you might need to give up a lot of personal information or pay high taxes on your crypto gains.

The Shifting Sands

Regulations are like the shifting sands of a desert; they can change under your feet when you least expect it. Let's say you invested in a cryptocurrency because it's legal and popular in your country. But then, out of the blue, the government decides to put new restrictions on it. Suddenly, the value of your investment might sink faster than a ship in a storm.

Why do governments change their stance? Well, they have their reasons. Maybe they're worried about illegal activities like money laundering or tax evasion. Or maybe they want to protect ordinary folks from losing money in a risky venture. Whatever the reason, when the rules change, it's like the wind changing direction while you're sailing — you need to adjust your sails quickly.

The Watchdogs

Governments have their own set of watchdogs to keep an eye on the financial markets, including crypto. In the United States, for example, you have the Securities and Exchange Commission (SEC). This agency can decide whether a cryptocurrency is a security, kind of like a stock, and therefore subject to certain rules and regulations. When these watchdogs bark, you better listen, because they have the power to freeze assets, shut down operations, and slap hefty fines on rule-breakers.

The Uncertain Future

No one has a crystal ball to see the future of crypto regulations. There are ongoing debates and discussions among lawmakers, and changes can happen at any time. Maybe they'll create new, friendly laws that boost the crypto market. Or maybe they'll enforce strict rules that make trading more complicated. It's all up in the air, which adds a layer of uncertainty to your crypto treasure hunt.

How to Navigate

So, what's a wise crypto adventurer to do? For starters, stay informed. Keep a keen eye on the news and always know the rules of the lands you're sailing in. If a law changes, you'll want to be the first to know so you can adjust your strategy. Secondly, diversify. Don't put all your treasures in one chest, so to speak. Having a mix of different investments can help you stay afloat even if one takes a nosedive.

And don't forget, if you're unsure about the regulatory environment, it might be a good idea to consult with experts, like financial advisors or legal professionals. They can help you navigate through the complex maze of rules and ensure you don't end up walking the plank.

In summary, regulatory risks are a critical part of the cryptocurrency landscape. Think of them as the changing tides and winds on your quest for treasure. Ignoring them could mean sailing right into a hurricane. But understanding them, and adjusting your sails accordingly, could help you reach the golden shores you seek.

So there you have it, the lowdown on regulatory risks. As you continue your journey in the crypto world, keep these risks in mind. They can't be avoided, but with the right knowledge and preparation, you can certainly manage them. After all, every good adventurer knows that danger is just part of the quest, but caution and wisdom are what bring you home with the treasure.

15.3 Security Risks

Security risks in the cryptocurrency world are like open doors in a house. If you leave them unattended, you're basically inviting trouble. With cybercrime on the rise and hackers becoming increasingly sophisticated, understanding security risks becomes a priority for anyone involved in cryptocurrency investments.

The Digital Wallet

One of the first things you'll do when you start investing in cryptocurrencies is set up a digital wallet. This wallet stores your cryptocurrencies, much like a bank account stores your money. However, unlike most bank accounts, if you lose access to your wallet, there's no customer service to call for help. If it gets hacked, your assets are gone, as if they've vanished into thin air.

Phishing Attacks

Phishing is a technique where someone tricks you into revealing sensitive information. For instance, you might get an email that looks like it's from your cryptocurrency exchange, asking you to confirm your login details. If you fall for it and enter your information, you've just given a hacker the keys to your wallet. It's essential to be cautious of unsolicited messages and verify the source before clicking on any links or giving out information.

Software Vulnerabilities

The world of cryptocurrency relies heavily on software. But all software has vulnerabilities or weak spots that can be exploited by hackers. Even big companies fall victim to this; we've all heard news stories about data breaches affecting millions of people. That's why it's essential to keep your software updated. Updates often contain fixes for known vulnerabilities.

Transaction Risks

In traditional banking, if you make an error in a transaction, there are ways to reverse it. In cryptocurrency, transactions are irreversible. Once you hit that "send" button, there's no turning back. If you sent your cryptocurrencies to the wrong address by mistake, they're lost.

Third-Party Risks

When you use exchanges, cloud wallets, or other third-party services, you're placing trust in them to secure your assets. But even these platforms aren't invincible. They can suffer from hacks, fraud, or even bad management. Do your research before trusting a third party. Look for platforms with a solid reputation and robust security measures.

Network Risks

Cryptocurrencies operate on decentralized networks. While these networks are generally secure, they aren't entirely free from risks. A well-coordinated attack could, in theory, gain control of the network, affecting transaction history and asset ownership. Though highly unlikely, it's not impossible.

Regulatory Environment

We've discussed how regulations can change, which could make it illegal to hold certain cryptocurrencies or use specific services. Failure to comply with these regulations could lead to frozen assets or legal consequences, adding another layer of risk to your investment.

Risk Management

Given all these risks, how do you keep your investments secure? The first step is education. Understand the technology and common scams, so you're less likely to fall victim. Use strong, unique passwords and enable two-factor authentication wherever possible. Always verify the legitimacy of services you use and keep an eye on the news for the latest vulnerabilities and fixes.

If you're storing large amounts of cryptocurrency, consider using a hardware wallet. These are physical devices that store your assets offline, making them immune to online hacking attempts.

And, of course, diversify your investments. Don't put all your eggs in one basket; spread your assets across various types of investments to minimize the impact if one of them goes south.

Finally, be prepared for the worst. Back up your wallet's essential information in secure, offline storage. Consider taking out insurance if available and applicable to your situation.

Conclusion

Security risks in the cryptocurrency market are a harsh reality we can't ignore. They are the walls and barriers that come with the financial freedom that cryptocurrencies offer. While they may seem daunting, understanding these risks and how to manage them can go a long way in securing your assets.

Whether you're new to the game or an experienced player, being aware of the security pitfalls can help you navigate this complicated yet rewarding landscape. The idea isn't to avoid risks entirely—that's impossible. Instead, aim to manage them intelligently. This way, you can invest with more confidence and fewer surprises.

15.4 How to Be a Responsible Investor

Investing is not just about making money; it's also about being responsible. Think of it like driving a car. Sure, you want to get to your destination, which in this case is financial success. But you also have to obey traffic laws, look out for other drivers, and take care of your car to get there safely. Similarly, being a responsible investor in the world of cryptocurrency involves following certain "rules of the road."

Understanding Your Investment

The first step to being responsible is understanding what you're investing in. If you buy a cryptocurrency without knowing its basics, you're driving blindfolded. Take the time to learn about what makes each cryptocurrency unique, how it's used, and its long-term potential. You wouldn't buy a car without checking its features and performance; don't invest in cryptocurrency without doing the same.

Risk Assessment

Investing always comes with risks. You've heard the phrase, "Don't put all your eggs in one basket." This wisdom applies to your investments too. Diversifying your portfolio—spreading your money across different types of assets—can help you mitigate risks. Before diving into an investment, evaluate its risk and see how it fits into your overall portfolio.

Security Measures

Your cryptocurrency investment needs strong security measures just like your home needs locks on its doors. Using strong passwords, enabling two-factor authentication, and keeping backups are good security practices. Regularly update your security measures to stay a step ahead of cybercriminals.

Staying Informed

The world of cryptocurrency is always changing. New developments can directly impact your investment. So, you must keep yourself updated. Subscribe to newsletters, follow industry experts on social media, and read credible news sources. Ignorance isn't bliss in investing; it's a recipe for failure.

Regular Monitoring

Investments are not a "set it and forget it" deal. Regularly monitor how your investments are performing. Are they living up to your expectations? Do you need to make adjustments? Much like you would get regular check-ups for your car, your investment portfolio needs regular evaluations.

Taxes and Regulations

A responsible investor also abides by the law. Cryptocurrency regulations vary from place to place, and failing to adhere to them can lead to legal issues. Be aware of the tax implications of your investments and report them correctly. When in doubt, consult a financial advisor or a legal expert.

Ethical Considerations

Believe it or not, your investment choices can have an ethical impact. Some cryptocurrencies are more energy-efficient than others; some have transparent business practices, and some contribute to social causes. Consider these factors when making an investment. Being responsible also means making ethical choices.

Know When to Step Back

Investing can be exciting, but it shouldn't be an emotional rollercoaster. Emotional decisions often lead to mistakes. Know when to step back, take a deep breath, and assess the situation logically. Sometimes, the best decision is to hold off on making any moves.

Learning from Mistakes

Nobody is perfect. You're likely to make mistakes along your investment journey. What sets a responsible investor apart is the ability to learn from these mistakes. Take them as lessons, not failures, and apply what you've learned to future decisions.

Long-Term Vision

Responsible investing isn't about making quick cash; it's about building sustainable wealth. Quick, short-term gains can be tempting, but they often come with high risks. Have a long-term vision for your investment portfolio. Set achievable goals and work steadily toward them, rather than chasing quick profits.

Taking Professional Advice

Sometimes, it's good to seek help, especially when you're dealing with complex financial products like cryptocurrencies. Financial advisors can offer expert opinions and help you make more informed decisions. It's like consulting a mechanic for car issues; you're getting expert advice to keep things running smoothly.

Your Well-being

Last but not least, being a responsible investor means taking care of yourself. Stress and anxiety can affect your decision-making abilities. Practice good mental health habits, maintain a work-life balance, and don't let the ups and downs of the market affect your overall well-being.

Conclusion

Being a responsible investor in the world of cryptocurrencies is about more than just aiming to make a profit. It involves understanding what you're investing in, staying informed, and following best practices to secure your investments. It also means being aware of the risks, obeying regulations, and, when necessary, seeking professional advice.

Investing might not come with a handbook, but that doesn't mean you should navigate it without guidelines. The more responsible you are, the more likely you are to succeed—not just in growing your wealth, but also in maintaining it securely for the long term. And remember, a smooth sea never made a skilled sailor, but a responsible sailor knows how to navigate even the choppiest waters.

15.5 Key Takeaways

Let's sum up what we've learned about being a responsible investor in the cryptocurrency space. Here are the main points to keep in mind:

1. **Understanding Your Investment:** Always know what you're investing in. Do your research to understand the fundamentals of each cryptocurrency.
2. **Risk Assessment:** Don't dive headfirst into any investment. Evaluate the risks and make sure it fits well with your overall financial strategy.
3. **Security Measures:** Protect your investments with strong security practices. Think strong passwords, two-factor authentication, and regular security updates.
4. **Staying Informed:** The crypto world is always evolving. Keep yourself updated with the latest news and trends.
5. **Regular Monitoring:** An investment portfolio needs regular check-ups. Review your investments frequently to make sure they're performing as you expect.
6. **Taxes and Regulations:** Always abide by the law. Know the tax implications of your investments and adhere to any regulations that apply.
7. **Ethical Considerations:** Your investment choices can have a broader impact. Consider the ethics of where you're putting your money.
8. **Know When to Step Back:** Emotional decisions often lead to mistakes. Know when it's time to pause and reevaluate.
9. **Learning from Mistakes:** Everyone makes mistakes; the key is learning from them to make better future decisions.
10. **Long-Term Vision:** Investing in cryptocurrency should be a marathon, not a sprint. Think long-term and set achievable goals.

11. **Professional Advice:** Don't shy away from seeking expert guidance. It can help you make more informed decisions.
12. **Your Well-being:** Being a responsible investor also means taking care of your mental and emotional well-being.

So there you have it. Being a responsible investor is a multifaceted role that goes beyond just trying to make quick profits. It's about being informed, vigilant, ethical, and law-abiding. It's a continuous learning process that requires your time and attention, but the benefits make it all worth it. Remember, the more responsible you are, the more likely you are to not just grow your wealth, but to keep it secure for the long term.

Section 16: Taxes and Regulations

Welcome to a topic that might not be the most exciting but is incredibly important—taxes and regulations in the world of cryptocurrencies. Yep, you heard it right. Just like everything else in life that involves money, the realm of cryptocurrencies isn't a lawless frontier. There are rules to follow, and the taxman will want his share.

Let's start with a simple truth: money makes the world go 'round. And where money flows, you can be certain that governments will want to know how it's being used, and if it's being used legally. That's where taxes and regulations come into play. Whether you are buying a candy bar, a car, or a cryptocurrency, the government wants its slice of the pie.

You might think, "Why do I need to worry about taxes when dealing with digital coins?" Good question! It turns out that governments across the globe are quite interested in your digital transactions. It's not just paper money and credit cards that catch their attention anymore. Cryptocurrencies have entered the spotlight, and as they've gained in popularity, so has the need for rules and regulations to govern their use.

Now, let's pause here and think about what taxes and regulations really mean for you, the individual investor. Sure, it can feel like a hassle to keep track of all the rules and file the necessary paperwork. But look at it from another angle. Regulations provide a sort of safety net for users. They set standards that help to weed out scams and illegal activities. And they create a more secure and trustworthy environment for everyone involved.

Taxes, while not everyone's favorite topic, serve a similar purpose. They fund public goods and services that we all benefit from, like roads, schools, and healthcare. When you pay your taxes honestly, you're contributing to the greater good of society. Even in the world of cryptocurrency, your financial choices have broader implications that go beyond just your personal gains or losses.

In the sections that follow, we'll dig deeper into the complexities surrounding cryptocurrency taxation. How are your gains or losses calculated? What happens if you neglect to report them? We'll also discuss the regulations that impact not just you but also the larger ecosystem of investors, developers, and institutions. What are the current laws? How might they change in the near future?

If you're reading this and already feeling overwhelmed, take a deep breath. Yes, the subject matter is complex, but we'll break it down into bite-sized pieces. Our aim is to provide you with the knowledge and tools you'll need to navigate this intricate landscape.

A word of caution: The material we'll cover isn't a substitute for professional tax or legal advice. The world of cryptocurrency is ever-changing, and what applies today may not be the case tomorrow. Therefore, it's essential to consult with professionals who can provide advice tailored to your individual circumstances.

In summary, understanding taxes and regulations is crucial if you're serious about investing in cryptocurrencies. Failure to comply can result in fines, penalties, and legal repercussions. Ignorance isn't an excuse when it comes to breaking the law. But don't worry, we're here to guide you through this often confusing and murky world.

By the end of this section, you'll have a strong grasp of what's expected of you as a responsible cryptocurrency investor in terms of taxes and regulations. So, let's roll up our sleeves and dive in. It's a topic that won't just save you from headaches but could also save you a lot of money and legal trouble in the long run.

16.1 Tax obligations

You've probably heard the saying, "Nothing is certain except death and taxes." Well, if Benjamin Franklin were alive today, he might add cryptocurrencies to that list. Because yes, even in the digital world of Bitcoin, Ethereum, and other cryptocurrencies, taxes are a very real thing.

So, what kind of tax obligations are we talking about? Let's start with the basics. Most governments look at cryptocurrencies not as real "money," but as property. That might sound weird, but it's an important distinction when tax season rolls around.

Capital Gains and Losses

Imagine you bought one Bitcoin for $5,000. A few months later, you're lucky, and the value of that Bitcoin goes up to $10,000. If you decide to sell it at that point, you've made a capital gain of $5,000. And guess what? That gain is taxable.

Now let's look at the flip side. Say you bought a Bitcoin for $10,000, but its value dropped to $5,000 and you decided to sell. Ouch! That's a capital loss of $5,000. The silver lining? You can use that loss to offset your gains, which could lower your tax bill.

Income Tax

But what if you didn't buy your cryptocurrency? What if you earned it, maybe through mining or as payment for a job? In that case, you'd have to pay income tax on the value of the cryptocurrency you received. It's treated just like getting paid in dollars or any other currency.

Keeping Records

Keeping accurate records is key when it comes to tax obligations. Document every transaction—buying, selling, trading, earning, or gifting cryptocurrency. Note the date, the value in your local currency at the time of the transaction, and any fees you had to pay.

Why is this so important? Because when tax season comes around, you'll need all this information to fill out your tax forms correctly. If you're missing information, it can cause delays, and you could even end up paying fines or penalties.

How to Report

To report your cryptocurrency transactions, you'll generally need to fill out specific tax forms, which vary from country to country. In the United States, for example, you'd use IRS Form 8949 and Schedule D. This might sound complicated, but there are software tools available that can help you compile this information.

Audits and Penalties

Here's where things get serious. Failing to report your cryptocurrency transactions is a risky move. It can trigger an audit, where the government takes a deep dive into your finances. And if they find out you haven't been honest, you could face some hefty penalties—or even legal action.

So, is it tempting to avoid all this tax stuff? Maybe. Is it worth the risk? Absolutely not.

Special Cases

Now, there are some special cases to be aware of. For example, if you only bought cryptocurrency but haven't sold or traded it, you generally don't have to report it on your taxes. However, as soon as you sell, trade, or earn more cryptocurrency, it becomes a taxable event.

Similarly, if you gift cryptocurrency, you might not have to pay taxes, but the person receiving the gift might have to when they sell or trade it.

Frequent Changes

One final point: tax laws are always changing, especially when it comes to new things like cryptocurrency. What this means for you is that you must stay up-to-date with the latest rules and regulations. That's another reason keeping accurate and detailed records is so crucial.

In summary, your adventures in the world of cryptocurrency come with responsibilities. The most important of these is understanding your tax obligations. Sure, it might not be the most exciting part of being a crypto investor, but it's definitely one of the most important.

Navigating the maze of tax rules can be tough, but it's a lot easier when you know what to expect. And by doing things the right way, you're not just protecting yourself; you're also contributing to a system that keeps everything running smoothly. After all, those tax dollars go towards things we all rely on, like roads, schools, and hospitals.

So keep good records, understand your obligations, and don't try to cheat the system. Because when it comes to taxes, it's always better to be safe than sorry.

16.2 Regulatory landscape

Just like a game has rules that players must follow, the world of cryptocurrency has its own set of rules, too. These rules are created by governments and other organizations, and they're what we call "regulations." Now, you might think regulations sound boring or complicated, but they're crucial to understanding how you can—and can't—use your cryptocurrency.

Why Regulations Exist

Let's start by talking about why these rules are even necessary. Cryptocurrencies offer a lot of freedom and opportunities, but they can also be used for things that are not so good, like fraud or illegal activities. Regulations help make sure everyone plays fair and square. They protect you, me, and everyone else involved.

Who Makes the Rules?

You might be wondering, who gets to make these rules? In the United States, it's usually government organizations like the Securities and Exchange Commission (SEC) or the Commodity Futures Trading Commission (CFTC). These organizations have the power to create regulations, enforce them, and punish those who break them.

What Do Regulations Cover?

These rules cover a whole lot of ground. Some regulations are about making sure companies that deal with cryptocurrencies are doing their business in a fair and honest way. Other rules might be about taxes, as we discussed earlier, or about how cryptocurrencies can be bought, sold, or traded.

KYC and AML

You may have heard the terms "KYC" and "AML" when dealing with cryptocurrencies. KYC stands for "Know Your Customer," and AML is "Anti-Money Laundering." These are rules that help make sure people are not using cryptocurrencies for illegal things like money laundering or fraud. When you use a cryptocurrency exchange, you're often required to provide some identification. That's these rules in action.

International Landscape

The interesting part about cryptocurrency is that it's not just a one-country thing; it's global. That means each country might have its own set of regulations. If you're in the United States, you have to follow U.S. rules, but if you're dealing with someone in, let's say, Europe, then European regulations might also come into play.

Risks of Non-Compliance

Here's where you have to be careful. Not following the rules could land you in some serious trouble. You could face fines, or in some severe cases, legal actions could be taken against you. That's why it's always important to know what the rules are and to make sure you're following them.

Changes and Updates

The world of cryptocurrency is like a fast-moving train. Things are always changing, and the same goes for regulations. Governments are continuously studying and evaluating how cryptocurrencies are being used, and they can update the rules at any time. It's your responsibility to stay updated with these changes. Ignorance is not an excuse that will work if you find yourself on the wrong side of the law.

Advocacy and Public Opinion

Believe it or not, you have a say in how these rules get made. Governments and organizations often seek public opinions before making new regulations. Sometimes they hold open discussions or invite comments from the public. Participating in these can give you a voice in how the world of cryptocurrency is shaped.

The Role of Legal Advisors

Because these rules can be complex, some people choose to consult with legal advisors who specialize in cryptocurrency. These professionals can help you understand your rights and responsibilities, and guide you through the maze of regulations.

Balancing Act

Regulations aren't just about setting limits; they're about creating a balanced and fair system where cryptocurrencies can be used safely and effectively. Too few regulations could lead to chaos and illegal activities, while too many could stifle innovation and freedom. It's a balancing act that governments are continually working on.

Personal Responsibility

In the end, understanding the regulatory landscape is your personal responsibility. Doing your research, keeping up to date with the latest rules, and even consulting with professionals can go a long way in ensuring you're playing by the rules.

Remember, being a responsible participant in the world of cryptocurrencies isn't just about making smart investment choices; it's also about understanding the law. The better you understand the regulatory landscape, the better equipped you'll be to navigate the exciting but complex world of cryptocurrencies. Knowledge is power, and in this case, it's also your best defense.

16.3 Key Takeaways

Importance of Regulations: Regulations are essential for maintaining fairness and security in the cryptocurrency market. They protect all the players involved and ensure that the game is played by the rules.

Who's In Charge: In the United States, organizations like the Securities and Exchange Commission (SEC) and the Commodity Futures Trading Commission (CFTC) are responsible for creating and enforcing cryptocurrency regulations.

Areas of Regulation: Regulations can cover a wide range of topics, from business practices of cryptocurrency companies to the taxes you have to pay on your crypto gains.

KYC and AML: "Know Your Customer" and "Anti-Money Laundering" are rules that help prevent illegal activities like fraud and money laundering. You'll encounter these when you sign up on cryptocurrency exchanges.

Global Complexity: Cryptocurrency is a worldwide phenomenon, and different countries have different rules. If you're dealing internationally, you may have to consider more than one set of regulations.

Risks: Not following the rules can result in severe penalties, ranging from fines to legal actions. So, it's always better to be informed and compliant.

Stay Updated: Regulations are not set in stone. They change as the cryptocurrency landscape evolves. It's your job to keep yourself updated on these changes.

Public Participation: Sometimes, the public gets to have a say in what new regulations should look like. Being a part of these discussions can give you a voice in the crypto community.

Legal Advisors: When in doubt, consulting with professionals who understand the legal landscape of cryptocurrencies can be very helpful.

Personal Responsibility: Ultimately, you're responsible for knowing and following the regulations related to your cryptocurrency activities. Knowledge is your most valuable asset in navigating this complex landscape.

By understanding these key takeaways, you arm yourself with the knowledge you need to be a responsible and informed participant in the fast-moving world of cryptocurrencies. The rules may seem complex, but they're there to create a level playing field for everyone. So, keep learning and stay aware. Your future self will thank you for it.

Part VI: Beyond Basics

Section 17: Smart Contracts and Decentralized Applications (DApps)

In the vast universe of cryptocurrency, two intriguing subjects often stand out like shining stars in the night sky: Smart Contracts and Decentralized Applications, also known as DApps. While these might sound like technical jargon from a far-off galaxy, they're actually here on Earth, transforming how we interact with the digital world. But what are they exactly? How do they work? Why should you even care? Hold tight; we're diving deep into these exciting topics in this section.

Let's start with Smart Contracts. Imagine you're buying a used car. Normally, you'd have to trust that the seller isn't giving you a lemon. With a smart contract, the transaction rules are written into lines of code. Once conditions are met, the contract self-executes. It's like having an unbiased robot referee, making sure both parties stick to the deal. It takes the guesswork and mistrust out of many situations, from simple transactions like buying and selling goods to complex ones like legal agreements and even voting systems.

Now, let's shift gears to Decentralized Applications or DApps. Traditional applications like Facebook or Gmail run on centralized servers owned by big companies. That means they control the data, and they make the rules. But what if we could take that control and distribute it among the users? Enter DApps, where no single entity has the reins. It's a democratic approach to software, powered by blockchain technology.

Why does this matter? Well, it turns out that both smart contracts and DApps have the potential to shake the very foundation of various industries. Think about it: No more middlemen in transactions, enhanced privacy, less red tape, and even more democratic systems for voting or community decisions. It sounds like a recipe for revolution, and in many ways, it is.

But like any tool, Smart Contracts and DApps have their own share of challenges and controversies. What happens if a smart contract has a flaw? What if a DApp is used for illegal activities? And how do these technologies fit into the existing laws and regulations? Don't worry; we'll unpack these questions and more, with clear explanations and real-world examples.

As you delve into this section, keep your thinking cap on. It's easy to get lost in the awe of what these technologies promise, but remember, the devil is in the details. From understanding how smart contracts are created to figuring out how to interact with DApps, knowledge is your guiding light. Whether you're a seasoned tech veteran or a curious newcomer, understanding Smart Contracts and DApps is your ticket to a more nuanced understanding of the cryptocurrency world.

Buckle up. We're about to embark on a fascinating journey, exploring the nooks and crannies of Smart Contracts and Decentralized Applications. It's a journey filled with potential, challenges, and a whole lot of learning. So, are you ready to dive in?

17.1 What Are They?

Alright, let's get down to business. You've probably heard the terms "Smart Contracts" and "Decentralized Applications," or DApps for short, tossed around a lot in conversations about cryptocurrency and blockchain. They sound fancy and complicated, but what exactly are they? Let's unravel this puzzle step by step.

Smart Contracts

First up, Smart Contracts. Imagine you're standing in the middle of a playground. On one side, you have Alice, who wants to sell her bicycle. On the other side, you have Bob, who wants to buy it. Normally, Alice and Bob would shake hands and agree on a price. But what if one of them doesn't keep their word? This is where a smart contract would come into play.

A Smart Contract is like a set of rules written in computer code. Instead of shaking hands, Alice and Bob would agree to these rules, which get recorded on the blockchain. It's like engraving their agreement on an unbreakable digital stone. Once the conditions are met—like Bob sending the agreed money—the smart contract self-executes. The bicycle ownership automatically switches from Alice to Bob. No need for a middleman, like a lawyer or a notary. The blockchain and smart contract handle it all.

You can think of smart contracts as digital agreements that can't be broken. They automatically do what they're supposed to do, without any need for human intervention. That's revolutionary because it removes the need for trust between parties. You don't have to trust that Alice or Bob will keep their word; you trust the contract. It's like having a digital referee that can't be bribed or fooled.

Decentralized Applications (DApps)

Now, let's move on to DApps, short for Decentralized Applications. Imagine your favorite video game. Normally, that game would run on a company's server. They control the rules, they control the data, and they make money from your time spent playing. But what if that control was spread out among the players themselves? That's the basic idea behind DApps.

In a DApp, there is no central authority or single point of control. The rules of the game are written in smart contracts, and the data is stored on a blockchain that everybody can see and verify. It's democracy in action, but in the digital realm. Any changes to the game would need to be agreed upon by a majority of players. Sounds fair, right?

This is a far cry from traditional applications like Facebook or Google Maps, where the company makes the rules, and you have to follow them. In a DApp, the users are in charge. This could mean more privacy, more fairness, and potentially, less cost as there's no central entity taking a big cut.

Why They Matter

Alright, you've got the basics down. But why should you care? The reason is pretty straightforward: these technologies could change how the world works. Smart contracts could make legal processes faster and cheaper. They could ensure that charity money goes exactly where it's promised. DApps could revolutionize everything from social media to online marketplaces. They could give people more control over their data and digital lives.

But it's not all sunshine and rainbows. Both smart contracts and DApps come with their own set of challenges. Smart contracts are only as good as the code they're written in. A tiny mistake could mean big trouble. And DApps, with their decentralized nature, could potentially be used for activities that aren't exactly above board, like illegal trading.

So, as we peel back the layers, keep your eyes wide open. These are powerful tools, but like any tool, they can be used for good or bad. The key is understanding what they are, how they work, and what their limitations are. In that way, you're not just following the crowd, but making informed decisions about whether and how to engage with these game-changing technologies.

There you have it—a rundown on what Smart Contracts and Decentralized Applications are, and a little taste of why they matter. And trust me, we're just scratching the surface here. So stay tuned, because the world of Smart Contracts and DApps is a deep and fascinating one, and we've got a lot more to explore.

17.2 Real-World Examples

Supply Chain Management

Let's kick off with something we all rely on but rarely think about: supply chains. Picture a supermarket. It's full of goods like fruits, veggies, and canned soup. Ever wonder how these items get from the farm or factory to the store? It's through a supply chain—a series of steps that moves products from point A to point B, then C, and so on.

In a traditional setup, each step is like a mini-mystery. Did the truck leave the farm on time? Is it stuck in traffic? When will the oranges arrive? These questions usually require calls, emails, and a lot of paperwork. But what if we could automate this with smart contracts?

Every time a truck leaves a farm, a smart contract could update the blockchain. As soon as it arrives at a warehouse, another update. This creates a real-time, unchangeable record that anyone in the chain can see. And remember, since it's on the blockchain, it's as solid as it gets. This reduces delays, prevents fraud, and makes sure you get fresh oranges in your shopping cart.

Property Sales

Think about the last time you bought a house—or maybe when your parents did. A mountain of paperwork, weeks of waiting, and loads of fees for real estate agents and lawyers, right? With smart contracts, that could be history.

A smart contract can store the details of the property, like its size, location, and price. When you agree to buy it, you and the seller both sign the digital contract. Money transfers automatically when all conditions are met. It's not just faster; it's transparent. No hidden fees, no last-minute changes. You see what you're getting into from the get-go.

Health Records

Healthcare is complicated. Just ask anyone who's tried to get their medical records transferred from one doctor to another. Paperwork gets lost, faxes don't go through, and sometimes it feels easier to just start from scratch.

Enter smart contracts and DApps. All your medical data could be stored securely on a blockchain. Need to switch doctors? A smart contract can transfer your records instantly, with your permission, of course. In an emergency, this could even save lives. Fast access to accurate data is crucial in medical care, and smart contracts can deliver just that.

Voting Systems

Voting is the cornerstone of any democracy, but it comes with challenges. Long lines at polling stations, worries about fraud, and even concerns about who's counting the votes. DApps have the potential to change this.

Imagine a voting system built on a blockchain. Each vote is a transaction, verified and recorded in real-time. Once the vote is in, it can't be changed or deleted, ensuring a fair process. Smart contracts can handle voter registration, identification, and even the final vote count. This could make voting as easy as checking your email.

Peer-to-Peer Lending

Borrowing money traditionally involves banks, credit checks, and interest rates that can make your head spin. Peer-to-peer lending platforms are simplifying this, but what if we add smart contracts to the mix?

You could lend money directly to someone else through a smart contract. This contract would outline terms like interest rates and repayment schedules. Once both parties agree, the contract executes automatically. Payments are made on time, every time—or the smart contract intervenes. Trust issues vanish, and you get a more democratic financial system.

Music and Content Distribution

Artists and creators often get a small slice of the revenue pie when it comes to selling their work online. Platforms like Spotify and YouTube take a significant cut. With DApps, this could change dramatically.

Artists could upload their music or videos directly to a decentralized platform. Every time someone listens or watches, a smart contract could ensure that the creator is paid immediately. No middlemen, no delayed payments, just a fair exchange between creator and consumer.

Challenges Ahead

We're getting a glimpse of a future reshaped by smart contracts and DApps. It's exciting, but it's not without hurdles. Smart contracts are, after all, written by humans—and humans make mistakes. A single error in code could have massive repercussions.

Similarly, DApps aren't a cure-all solution. They might be resistant to censorship, but they can also be harder to regulate. What happens when a DApp is used for illegal activities? It's a complex problem, and the answers aren't straightforward.

Final Thoughts

The applications of smart contracts and DApps stretch as far as the imagination can go. These are tools with the power to rebuild foundations and shift paradigms, but like any powerful tool, they have their limitations and risks. Understanding those limits is key to using these technologies wisely and effectively.

So there you have it. Real-world examples that pull smart contracts and DApps out of the realm of abstract tech jargon and into the concrete, tangible world we live in. And this, believe it or not, is just the beginning. As these technologies evolve, who knows what new applications we'll see? One thing's for sure: it's going to be a fascinating journey, and it's one that's worth keeping an eye on.

17.3 Key Takeaways

Real-world Impact: Smart contracts and decentralized applications (DApps) are not just tech buzzwords. They have the potential to revolutionize various industries, from supply chain management to healthcare.

Transparency and Security: One of the biggest benefits of using smart contracts and DApps is the unparalleled transparency and security they offer. They use blockchain technology, which is almost impossible to tamper with, providing a level of trust that traditional systems can't match.

Automated Efficiency: Smart contracts automate processes that used to require a lot of human intervention. This can drastically speed things up and reduce the chance of errors or fraud.

Accessibility: DApps, especially in the context of peer-to-peer lending or content distribution, can democratize access to various services. They can bypass traditional gatekeepers like banks and media companies, allowing direct interactions between users.

Legal and Regulatory Challenges: As promising as these technologies are, they do raise new legal and ethical questions. From coding errors to regulatory oversight, there's a lot that still needs to be figured out.

User Responsibility: With great power comes great responsibility. The decentralized nature of these technologies means that you're often your own bank, lawyer, or contract manager. While this cuts out middlemen, it also means you need to be extra cautious and informed.

Future Potential: The examples we discussed are just the tip of the iceberg. As the technology matures, we can expect to see even more innovative applications that could further transform our day-to-day lives.

Limitations and Risks: Like any technology, smart contracts and DApps have their limitations. Coding errors can have significant consequences, and the technology itself can be used for both good and bad. Awareness of these limitations is crucial for responsible use.

So there you have it. Smart contracts and DApps are more than just exciting new technologies; they are tools with the potential to reshape our world. But with that potential comes a host of questions, challenges, and responsibilities. Being aware of these is the first step towards harnessing their full potential responsibly.

Section 18: Initial Coin Offerings (ICOs) and Tokens

We've journeyed through the world of cryptocurrencies, smart contracts, and even peeked into how these technologies are affecting real-world systems. But let's not stop here. There's another intriguing aspect of the crypto universe that's worth exploring: Initial Coin Offerings, or ICOs for short, and Tokens. You can think of ICOs like the grand openings of new shops, but instead of cutting a ribbon, they're offering tokens—digital assets—as a way to raise money.

In simple terms, ICOs are fundraising events for new projects in the blockchain space. Imagine you have an idea for a new kind of digital service, like a social network where users can earn money for their posts. You've got the idea, you've got the ambition, but you don't have the money to make it happen. That's where ICOs come in. They're a way to invite people to invest in your project, and in return, these people receive tokens they can use within your service or sell to others.

But why should you care? Well, ICOs have the potential to be massively profitable, but they also carry their own set of unique risks. Imagine you buy a ticket to a magic show, expecting dazzling performances. But what if the magician turns out to be an amateur and the show falls flat? You might feel like you wasted your time and money. ICOs can be similar. They promise a world of opportunity, but not all deliver on those promises.

And that's where tokens come in. Tokens are a bit like shares in a company or tickets to an event. Owning a token can give you voting rights in how a project is run or can be used to access certain services within a platform. There are even tokens that represent real-world assets like gold or real estate. Imagine owning a tiny piece of a famous painting and getting a share of the profits when it's rented out for exhibitions.

But here's the catch—tokens are also a very new concept. They're not as regulated as traditional stocks, and the market for them can be wild and unpredictable. It's a landscape full of promise and innovation, but it's also a terrain where you can easily trip and fall if you're not careful. So, tread cautiously.

We can't ignore the fact that ICOs and tokens have led to some controversies. There have been scams and projects that failed, causing people to lose their investments. That's why it's crucial to be aware of the risks involved, to understand what exactly you're investing in, and to know how to protect yourself from the not-so-great actors in this space. This isn't just a gold rush; it's more like venturing into a dense forest, where both treasures and traps await.

In this section, we will peel back the layers of ICOs and tokens. We'll look at why they are essential in the cryptocurrency world, how to evaluate them, and what you need to be cautious about. We'll discuss the different types of tokens, how they work, and why they matter. It's a complex subject, but understanding it can offer you another level of insight into the fascinating, fast-paced world of cryptocurrencies.

The road ahead is packed with information, cautionary tales, and critical tools to help you navigate this evolving space. As always, the aim is not just to inform but to equip you with the knowledge to make wise choices in the realm of ICOs and tokens.

So, if you're ready to delve deeper into this cutting-edge area of blockchain technology, let's get started. Remember, as exciting as it all might seem, it's crucial to keep a balanced perspective. The world of ICOs and tokens is neither all doom and gloom nor a guaranteed ticket to riches. Like any financial venture, it comes with its share of opportunities and pitfalls.

Consider this your map and compass for the journey ahead. Keep your wits about you, and let's explore what ICOs and tokens have to offer.

18.1 What is an ICO?

Initial Coin Offerings, or ICOs, might sound like fancy jargon you'd hear in a business meeting, but don't let that scare you off. At its core, an ICO is a modern way for new businesses, mostly those working with blockchain technology, to get the funding they need. It's like a big, digital fundraiser for brand-new projects. Instead of offering stock shares like companies do on Wall Street, these projects offer something called tokens.

You can think of tokens like rare trading cards. People buy them because they believe those cards will be valuable someday. In the same way, when a new project offers an ICO, they're selling tokens because they need money to get their ideas off the ground. The idea is, if the project becomes successful, those tokens you bought will become more valuable. You can either use them on the platform you invested in or sell them to someone else who wants them.

But why "Initial" Coin Offering? The word "initial" here is similar to how it's used in "Initial Public Offering" or IPO, which is a way traditional companies raise money by going public and selling shares. An ICO is the first time a new crypto project is offering its tokens to the public.

To break it down, here's how an ICO typically works:

1. **The Whitepaper:** Before anything else, the team behind the project releases a whitepaper. This is a document that outlines what the project aims to do, how it's different from others, and how it plans to achieve its goals. This whitepaper is crucial; it's like a blueprint or a game plan.
2. **Announcement:** The project then announces the ICO publicly, usually through social media, forums, and websites where people interested in cryptocurrencies hang out. This is the project's chance to generate buzz and get people interested in what they're doing.
3. **Token Sale:** On a predetermined date, the ICO officially kicks off. This is when you can buy the project's tokens. Often, there's a set amount of tokens available and a set period during which you can buy them.
4. **Funding and Distribution:** People buy tokens by sending cryptocurrencies like Bitcoin or Ethereum to a specific address. Once the ICO is over, the project distributes the tokens to the investors.
5. **Exchange Listing:** After the ICO, the next step is usually to get the tokens listed on cryptocurrency exchanges. This is important because if people can't buy or sell your tokens easily, they're not very useful.

Sounds straightforward, right? Well, yes and no. ICOs offer an exciting opportunity for innovation and can turn small investments into big gains. However, they are also extremely risky. In the past, there have been ICOs that raised millions of dollars and then vanished, leaving investors with worthless tokens.

You've got to be cautious. Think of it like buying a ticket for a rocket ship to a newly discovered planet. That ticket could lead to a world of new opportunities, or it could turn out to be a one-way trip to nowhere. That's why understanding the ins and outs of what an ICO is, is crucial before you decide to invest.

For one, regulations around ICOs aren't as strict as those around traditional investments, like stocks or bonds. This lack of regulation is a double-edged sword. On one hand, it allows for more freedom and innovation. On the other hand, it opens the door for dishonest people to take advantage of investors.

So, you have to dig deep. Always read the whitepaper, research the team behind the project, and maybe even consult financial experts. The more informed you are, the better your chances of not getting burned. And don't invest money you can't afford to lose. Investing in an ICO is a gamble, not a guarantee.

At this point, you might be wondering whether all ICOs are risky ventures where you could lose all your money. The answer is no, but it's essential to know that the risk is there. However, there are also plenty of success stories, projects that have gone on to revolutionize various industries, making their early investors very happy in the process.

By now, you should have a good grasp of what an ICO is—a fundraising tool in the cryptocurrency world that can be both promising and risky. In this complex landscape, being informed is your best defense and your path to making decisions that you won't regret.

This knowledge is more than just trivia; it's a tool, a lens through which you can better understand the ever-evolving world of digital currencies. It's all about equipping you with the knowledge you need to navigate the winding and often unpredictable road of cryptocurrencies.

So, hold on tight. We're diving deeper into this world, one token at a time. And as always, tread carefully, ask questions, and keep learning.

18.2 How to Participate

So, you've heard about Initial Coin Offerings (ICOs) and the allure of new projects offering tokens that could be the next big thing. Your curiosity is piqued, but how exactly do you get in on the action? Participating in an ICO isn't a casual walk in the park; it involves several careful steps and deep consideration.

Step 1: Do Your Homework

Just like you wouldn't buy a car without doing some research, you shouldn't jump into an ICO without knowing what you're getting into. Remember that document called a "whitepaper" we talked about earlier? Start there. Read it closely. Does the project solve a real problem? Does it have a unique approach? Also, investigate the team behind the project. Do they have experience in the field? Have they successfully launched other ventures?

Step 2: Find the ICO

You may find out about ICOs from various sources: online forums, social media, or websites dedicated to tracking new ICOs. Once you identify an ICO that looks promising, check its official website. That's where you'll find all the details like the start and end date for the token sale, the total number of tokens, and how to register.

Step 3: Get Your Wallet Ready

Most ICOs accept major cryptocurrencies like Bitcoin or Ethereum. You'll need to set up a digital wallet compatible with the cryptocurrency you plan to use for buying tokens. Make sure it's a wallet where you control your private keys because you'll need them to access your tokens later.

Step 4: Register and Get Verified

Many ICOs require you to complete a process known as Know Your Customer (KYC). It's a verification method to make sure you are who you say you are. You may need to upload identification documents like a passport or driver's license. This process could take some time, so don't leave it to the last minute.

Step 5: Participate in the Sale

Once you're registered and your wallet is ready, you can participate in the ICO when it opens. You'll send cryptocurrency from your wallet to the ICO's wallet address. Make absolutely sure you're sending it to the correct address. A mistake here could mean your funds are lost forever.

Step 6: Receive Your Tokens

After the ICO is over, the project will distribute the tokens to all participants. How and when this happens will be specified by the project, often in their whitepaper or on their website. You'll use your digital wallet to receive these tokens.

Step 7: Stay Involved

Your involvement shouldn't end once you receive your tokens. Keep tabs on the project. Are they meeting their milestones? Are they active on social media and forums? Have they listed their token on cryptocurrency exchanges? If the answer to these questions is yes, it's a good sign.

Risks and Precautions

At this point, it's crucial to discuss the risks associated with ICOs. Participating in an ICO can be similar to entering a maze. It can be exciting, but you can also get lost if you're not careful. Here are some risks and how to mitigate them:

Scams: As we mentioned earlier, not all ICOs are legitimate. Some are outright scams designed to take your money and disappear. Thoroughly research to avoid falling victim.

Regulatory Risks: The rules and regulations about ICOs can vary from one country to another, and they're constantly changing. Make sure you're aware of the legal landscape before you invest.

Technical Issues: Technology isn't always perfect. There can be bugs, errors, or security vulnerabilities that might affect your investment. Always make sure you're using secure and reliable platforms.

Market Risk: Even if an ICO is legitimate, there's no guarantee that its tokens will increase in value. The cryptocurrency market is volatile, and you should be prepared for ups and downs.

Liquidity Risks: After you've received your tokens, you might find that you can't easily sell them. They need to be listed on an exchange, and even then, there may not be a lot of buyers.

Safety First

Above all, never invest more than you can afford to lose. The world of ICOs is filled with both promise and peril. If you're not cautious, you could end up on the losing end. So, always make sure you've done exhaustive research, understood the risks, and prepared for different outcomes.

Let's put it this way: if ICOs were a game, it would be one where the stakes are high, but so are the rewards. You're not just tossing a coin and hoping for the best; you're making informed decisions based on thorough understanding and analysis.

By following these steps and being aware of the associated risks, you're not just throwing darts in the dark. You're aiming with precision, even though there's no guarantee of hitting the bullseye. In the unpredictable world of ICOs, knowledge is your compass, caution is your shield, and due diligence is your sword.

As you journey through the land of ICOs, carry these tools with you. They won't make the path any less rocky, but they'll give you a better shot at navigating through without stumbling. Remember, every ICO is a story waiting to unfold, and by participating wisely, you become part of that narrative—either as a cautionary tale or as a success story. Choose wisely.

18.3 Key Takeaways

Navigating the world of Initial Coin Offerings (ICOs) can feel like walking through a maze. But with the right knowledge, you can find your way and maybe even discover something valuable. Here are the key takeaways for how to participate in an ICO and what to be cautious about:

Research is King

Before jumping in, research is your most valuable tool. Read the whitepaper, investigate the team, and make sure the project has a unique approach to solving a real problem. A little time spent researching could save you from a lot of trouble later on.

Get Your Wallet Ready

You'll need a digital wallet compatible with the cryptocurrency you plan to use. This isn't just any wallet; it should be one where you control your private keys. This is crucial for securing your investment.

Know Your Customer (KYC)

KYC isn't just an annoying formality; it's a required step for many ICOs. Be prepared to verify your identity by submitting identification documents like a passport or driver's license.

The Steps to Participation

Once you've done your homework, have your wallet ready, and completed the KYC process, you're all set to participate. You'll send your chosen cryptocurrency to the ICO's wallet address. This is a one-way street, so double-check that address.

Stay Engaged

After the ICO, your responsibility isn't over. Track the project's progress. Are they reaching milestones? Have they listed their token on an exchange? Your continued attention can help you decide if you want to hold or sell your tokens later on.

Understand the Risks

Scams: Not all ICOs are what they appear to be. Be vigilant.

Regulatory Risks: Laws surrounding ICOs are still evolving. Know what applies to you.

Technical Issues: Mistakes and vulnerabilities can happen, affecting your investment.

Market Risks: The value of your tokens could rise, but it could also fall. Be prepared.

Liquidity Risks: Even after getting your tokens, you might find that selling them isn't straightforward.

Caution Above All

Never invest more than you're willing to lose. ICOs offer no guarantees. Treat each one as a risk but also as an opportunity. The cryptocurrency world is still young, and investing in it is like investing in any start-up: filled with both potential and peril.

Remember, when it comes to ICOs, your journey can either be a lesson for others on what not to do or a blueprint for how to do it right. The choice is yours. Armed with these key takeaways, you're better equipped to make that choice a wise one.

Section 19: The Future of Cryptocurrencies and Blockchain

The future is a mysterious place. We can't predict it with complete accuracy, but we can think about the possibilities. Imagine being a sailor on the verge of discovering new lands. You have your compass, your map, and a skilled crew. Yet, despite your best preparations, the ocean is vast and filled with unknowns. In a way, the future of cryptocurrencies and blockchain technology feels much the same.

Right now, we stand at the edge of an era. Think about how the internet changed the way we live, work, and communicate. It revolutionized our world. Cryptocurrencies and blockchain have the same kind of potential. They could reshape economies, redefine industries, and bring new ways of doing things that we haven't even thought of yet. Exciting? Absolutely. But just like those early explorers, we have to be cautious and well-prepared. The waters ahead could be choppy, and there might be storms we'll have to weather.

Cryptocurrencies like Bitcoin, Ethereum, and many others have proven that they're more than just a passing trend. They've overcome doubts, regulatory hurdles, and technological challenges. People are starting to take them seriously, not just as investments but also as a way to bring financial services to those who've been left out by traditional banking systems. Think about it—someone in a rural village can now have the same access to financial services as someone in a bustling city, all thanks to this technology. The implications are massive and far-reaching.

Blockchain, the technology that makes cryptocurrencies possible, has its own set of possibilities. Imagine a world where you don't have to worry about someone stealing your identity, where voting in elections can be done securely from your phone, or where you can track where your food comes from, right down to the farm. These things may sound like they're from a science fiction novel, but they're all within the realm of what blockchain could make possible.

However, as with all things that have the power to bring monumental changes, there are challenges and obstacles. Governments are still figuring out how to regulate cryptocurrencies. Scammers are coming up with new ways to deceive people. Technological limitations could slow down or even halt progress. We need to be aware of these challenges, and be prepared to face them head-on.

But let's not forget about you, the individual. The way you interact with money, the way you do business, and the way you live your daily life could all be affected by these developments. Whether you're an investor, a business owner, or just someone who wants to keep up with the times, understanding what's on the horizon is essential. The choices you make today could have a significant impact on your future.

So, as we venture into this new territory, what should we expect? What are the risks, and what are the rewards? Will cryptocurrencies replace traditional money? Will blockchain disrupt the way we do things across various sectors, from healthcare to real estate? In this section, we're going to examine some of these questions and ponder the possible futures that lie ahead.

It's an exciting journey, but it's also a serious one. So, pull out your compass and ready your crew. We're sailing into the future, and it's going to be a voyage worth taking.

19.1 Upcoming Developments

When you look at a seed, it's hard to imagine the giant tree it might become. But given the right conditions—sunlight, water, and a little bit of time—that tiny seed can grow into something truly remarkable. The same goes for technologies like cryptocurrencies and blockchain. What we see now are the early stages, like seeds just starting to sprout. But what could they grow into? Let's explore some of the upcoming developments that experts are talking about.

1. Scalability

Remember standing in a long line at a theme park, waiting for your turn on a roller coaster? No one likes waiting. Well, some cryptocurrencies have a similar problem. They're popular, but when too many people use them at once, things slow down. Experts are working on ways to make cryptocurrencies faster and able to handle more transactions. This is known as "scalability," and it's a big deal. The quicker and more efficient these systems become, the more people will use them.

2. Environmental Concerns

We all know we have to take care of our planet. Cryptocurrencies, especially Bitcoin, have been criticized for using too much electricity. Imagine powering thousands of houses for a whole day—that's how much energy some of these systems can use. So, there's a push to make cryptocurrencies more "green." Future developments might include new methods of verifying transactions that use less energy.

3. Regulation

Laws and rules aren't always fun, but they're essential to making sure things work properly and fairly. Right now, governments around the world are figuring out how to regulate cryptocurrencies. What does this mean for you? Well, as these technologies become more mainstream, they'll also become safer and more reliable. But remember, new laws could also bring challenges. It's a bit like adding guardrails to a highway—safer, but also limiting in some ways.

4. Improved Security

Hackers are like the burglars of the digital world. They're always looking for ways to steal valuable things, including cryptocurrencies. Security experts are in a constant battle with these digital thieves, working to build stronger locks and better alarms. Expect future cryptocurrencies and blockchain systems to be even more secure than they are now.

5. Financial Inclusion

Think about people in far-off places, where there are no banks or ATMs. Cryptocurrencies can be a game-changer for them. With just a smartphone, they could have access to the kinds of financial services that many of us take for granted. This is known as "financial inclusion," and it could lift millions of people out of poverty.

6. Adoption by Big Companies

More and more big companies are starting to accept cryptocurrencies. Imagine buying your next car or even your groceries using Bitcoin or another digital currency. This would make cryptocurrencies more useful in everyday life, not just as something to invest in.

7. Integration with Existing Systems

Right now, cryptocurrencies and traditional money systems are like two separate roads. But what if they were connected by bridges? In the future, we might see better integration between cryptocurrencies and traditional banks, making it easier for people to move their money around.

8. Smart Contracts and Decentralized Apps

We talked about these before, remember? Smart contracts are like digital agreements that automatically enforce themselves. And decentralized apps (DApps) run on a network of computers instead of just one. These technologies could change how we do everything, from buying a house to streaming music.

9. Public Awareness

Knowledge is power. The more people know about cryptocurrencies and blockchain, the more they'll use them. Education and public awareness are key. You might start seeing classes in schools or special programs on TV that help people understand these technologies.

10. The Unknown Factor

And then, there's the unknown. Just like explorers can't predict what they'll find in uncharted lands, we can't predict all the twists and turns that the future holds for cryptocurrencies and blockchain. New technologies could emerge, laws could change, and public opinion could shift. That's what makes this journey so intriguing.

We stand on the brink of a series of changes that could reshape our world. These are not just upgrades or tweaks, but potential revolutions in how we deal with money, contracts, and trust. The seeds have been planted, and they are starting to sprout. The question isn't just what they'll grow into, but how we'll adapt and grow with them.

So, as we look forward, it's essential to keep learning and stay informed. The landscape is changing, and you'll want to be prepared for whatever comes next. Like a gardener tending to a young sapling, we have the opportunity to nurture these technologies, to help them grow into something that benefits us all. And that makes this not just an exciting time but an important one as well.

19.2 Government and Regulation

Imagine you're at a busy intersection in your town or city. Cars are zipping by, people are crossing the street, and everyone seems to know what they're doing. Why? Because there are rules—stoplights, crosswalks, and speed limits—that help everyone move smoothly and safely. Now, think about the world of cryptocurrencies and blockchain. It's like a bustling intersection, but with fewer rules. That's where governments and regulations come into play.

The Early Days: Wild West

In the early years of cryptocurrencies, things were a bit like the Wild West. People were excited and intrigued, rushing to get a piece of the action. There were few rules, and that made it thrilling but also risky. Think of it as a busy marketplace with no one overseeing the quality of goods or watching out for scams. A lot could go wrong.

The Need for Regulation

As cryptocurrencies grew more popular, so did the problems. Scams became common. Hackers found ways to steal funds, and some people used digital money for illegal activities. It was clear that rules were needed, just like traffic lights at a busy intersection. Regulation isn't about crushing innovation or making things boring. It's about safety and fairness.

Government Involvement: A Mixed Bag

Not all governments view cryptocurrencies in the same way. Some countries have welcomed them with open arms, seeing the potential benefits for their economies. Others have been more cautious, imposing restrictions or even banning certain activities. In some cases, the government itself has launched a digital currency. These different approaches create a patchwork of rules that can be confusing to navigate.

Categories of Regulation

Let's break down the types of regulations we might see:

1. **Consumer Protection:** These rules aim to keep people safe. They could require companies to keep better records or to have security measures that protect against hacks.
2. **Anti-Money Laundering (AML) and Combating the Financing of Terrorism (CFT):** These regulations aim to prevent illegal activities like money laundering, where people try to hide the source of their money, and terrorist financing.
3. **Taxation:** You can't escape taxes, not even in the digital world. Governments want their share, and they're working on ways to tax cryptocurrency transactions.
4. **Licensing:** Some places require cryptocurrency exchanges—the websites where you can buy and sell digital money—to get a license to operate.
5. **Initial Coin Offerings (ICOs):** Remember those? Governments are particularly interested in regulating ICOs to make sure they're fair and not just schemes to scam people out of their money.

Impact on Innovation

Rules and innovation are often seen as enemies, but they don't have to be. Good regulations can help innovations grow in a way that's safe and beneficial for everyone. However, too many rules or poorly thought-out ones can stifle creativity. It's a delicate balance.

Global Coordination: A Work in Progress

In an ideal world, all countries would work together to create a set of rules that apply everywhere. That would make things much easier for companies and users alike. However, we're not there yet. Different countries have their own views and interests, making international coordination challenging.

The Role of Community and Self-Regulation

Sometimes, the community around a particular cryptocurrency takes the lead in setting rules. This is known as self-regulation and can be an effective way to address issues more quickly than waiting for government action.

Transparency and Accountability

One of the promises of blockchain is greater transparency—the idea that all transactions are recorded and can be checked by anyone. This could be a boon for regulators, making it easier to catch fraud and other illegal activities.

Ethical Considerations

Last but not least, we have to think about the ethical side of things. How do we make sure that cryptocurrencies and blockchain are used for good and not bad? Regulation can play a role here, guiding the technology in a direction that benefits society as a whole.

As we move forward, the relationship between governments, regulations, and cryptocurrencies will be one of the key stories to watch. Will the rules help or hinder the growth of this exciting new world? Only time will tell.

To navigate this evolving landscape, you'll need to be informed and adaptable, just like a driver learning to maneuver through a newly constructed intersection. Regulations aren't roadblocks but signposts, helping us find our way in a complex world. So keep your eyes open and your mind engaged. The road ahead may be uncertain, but it's also full of potential. And the decisions we make now—both as individuals and as a society—will shape what comes next.

19.3 Adoption and Acceptance

Think of a time when something new appeared on the scene and made a big splash. Maybe it was the first time you heard about smartphones, or when streaming services like Netflix became popular. At first, not everyone jumped on board. Some people were skeptical, wondering if these new things were just fads that would quickly fade away. Others were eager to give them a try, loving the convenience and the new possibilities they offered. Over time, more and more people started to use these new technologies, until they became part of our everyday lives.

The Initial Skepticism

When cryptocurrencies and blockchain first came onto the scene, they were met with a lot of skepticism. People questioned whether digital currencies could ever replace traditional money. They wondered about the security of these new technologies and whether they could be trusted. And they weren't wrong to have those concerns. New things often come with risks and uncertainties.

Early Adopters: The Brave Few

Then there were the early adopters—the people who saw the potential in cryptocurrencies and blockchain from the get-go. These are the individuals and businesses who were willing to take a chance, to dive into uncharted waters. They started using cryptocurrencies for a variety of things, from making online purchases to transferring money across borders without having to pay high fees. Businesses began to explore the possibilities of blockchain for tracking goods and ensuring the integrity of their supply chains.

Crossing the Chasm: From Niche to Mainstream

You've probably heard the phrase "Crossing the chasm." It's a term used to describe the jump from a small group of early adopters to a larger, mainstream audience. For cryptocurrencies and blockchain, crossing this chasm hasn't been easy. There have been setbacks, like security breaches and scams. And there have been challenges, like the lack of understanding among the general public about what cryptocurrencies and blockchain are and how they work.

Breaking Down Barriers

Several barriers have stood in the way of broader adoption and acceptance. Here are a few:

1. **Lack of Understanding:** A lot of people find cryptocurrencies and blockchain confusing. They're not sure how they work or why they should use them.
2. **Regulatory Uncertainty:** The varying rules and regulations from one place to another can make it hard for people to know what's allowed and what's not.
3. **Security Concerns:** Stories of hacking and fraud have made many people wary.
4. **Volatility:** The value of cryptocurrencies can swing wildly from one day to the next, which can be off-putting.
5. **Accessibility:** In some parts of the world, people don't have easy access to the technology needed to use cryptocurrencies.

The Turning Tide

Despite these challenges, things are starting to change. Major companies are beginning to accept cryptocurrencies as a form of payment. Governments are exploring the use of blockchain for things like voting systems and identity verification. Educational initiatives are being rolled out to help people better understand these technologies. And advancements are being made to improve security and reduce volatility.

A Multiplicity of Uses

The applications of cryptocurrencies and blockchain go beyond just buying things online. They're being used in healthcare to secure medical records. They're being used in real estate to simplify the buying and selling process. They're even being used in humanitarian efforts, enabling quick and transparent distribution of aid.

The Role of the Media

The media has played a significant part in shaping public perception. News stories about the highs and lows of cryptocurrency markets, or about major companies adopting blockchain, have helped to drive interest and discussion.

A Future Not So Far Away

As we look ahead, it's clear that cryptocurrencies and blockchain are not just passing trends. They're technologies with the potential to bring about meaningful changes in the way we live and work. Just like smartphones and streaming services, they may soon become so integrated into our daily routines that we can't imagine life without them.

The Power of Collective Choice

But here's the thing: the future isn't set in stone. It's shaped by the choices we make. Each time someone decides to use a cryptocurrency or implement a blockchain solution, they're casting a vote for the kind of future they want to see—one that's more open, transparent, and equitable.

So, what will it be? Will cryptocurrencies and blockchain join the ranks of revolutionary technologies that changed the world, or will they remain on the fringes, never quite breaking through to the mainstream? The answer lies in the hands of people like you and me. Our choices, big and small, will determine what happens next. And the path we choose will be one for the history books, telling future generations about the time when a new technology appeared on the scene, and the world was never the same again.

19.4 Challenges Ahead

Every story of innovation and progress comes with its own set of challenges. Imagine a road stretching out in front of you. It's not a straight path; it has bumps, twists, and turns. Just like that road, the journey of cryptocurrencies and blockchain is full of obstacles. But remember, challenges aren't roadblocks; they're opportunities to learn, adapt, and grow stronger.

The Weight of Regulation

One of the big concerns that loom over the world of cryptocurrencies and blockchain is regulation. Think of regulation as a set of rules that say what you can and can't do. While rules are important for keeping things safe and fair, they can also slow down progress. Governments around the world are still figuring out how to regulate these new technologies. Some countries are welcoming, while others are cautious or even hostile. This mixed bag of approaches makes it tough for businesses and individuals to navigate the terrain.

Technical Limitations

Believe it or not, even the most advanced technologies have their limits. One of the big talking points in the crypto world is scalability. That's a fancy word for how well a system can grow and manage more and more users. Right now, some of the most well-known cryptocurrencies have issues with slow transaction times and high fees when too many people try to use them. Technologists are working day and night to find solutions, but there's still a long way to go.

Security and Trust: Building the Fort

Even if a fortress looks strong from the outside, one small weakness can make it vulnerable. The same is true for the digital world. Security concerns are a major challenge. We've heard stories of hackers stealing millions of dollars in cryptocurrency or breaking into blockchain systems. This scares people and makes them hesitate to join the crypto world. To overcome this, ongoing efforts are being made to bolster security, but it's a constant cat-and-mouse game with hackers.

Economic Instability: The Roller Coaster Ride

If you've ever been on a roller coaster, you know the feeling of ups and downs, twists and turns. The economic aspects of cryptocurrencies can be just like that. The value can skyrocket one day and plummet the next. This volatility is exciting for some but frightening for others, especially those who see their life savings go up in smoke. Stability is something that will have to be addressed for mainstream adoption.

Societal Hesitation: Breaking Old Habits

Old habits die hard. People are used to dealing with traditional money and are often wary of what they don't understand. Despite growing awareness, many still view cryptocurrencies and blockchain as complicated or risky. It's like being offered a new type of food; unless you know it's safe and tasty, you're probably not going to try it.

Environmental Concerns: The Planet's Bill

Imagine leaving all the lights in your house on, all day, every day. That's going to be one hefty electric bill, not to mention the strain it puts on our planet's resources. Some cryptocurrencies require massive amounts of energy to maintain. The environmental impact has been a hot topic and a point of criticism. Alternatives are being explored, but finding a solution that's both efficient and eco-friendly is a daunting task.

The Information Gap: Education and Awareness

Even though we live in an age of information, not everyone has access to the right kind of knowledge. A lot of people hear about cryptocurrencies and blockchain through the grapevine, and not all that information is accurate or reliable. Spreading accurate knowledge is crucial for adoption and acceptance.

Social and Ethical Implications: The Moral Compass

Like any technology, cryptocurrencies and blockchain can be used for both good and bad. They can offer financial freedom but can also be used for illegal activities. Striking a balance between innovation and ethical concerns is a complex challenge.

Future-Proofing: Ready for What's Next

The technology world moves at a breakneck pace. What's hot today might be forgotten tomorrow. For cryptocurrencies and blockchain to have a long-lasting impact, they need to be adaptable and ready to evolve. Future-proofing these technologies against what's to come is an ongoing endeavor.

The Road Ahead: A Journey, Not a Destination

So, what's the takeaway? The journey of cryptocurrencies and blockchain is far from over. There are challenges ahead, no doubt about it. But challenges are part of any journey. They make us question, rethink, and strive for better solutions.

As more people from different walks of life get involved, as governments and institutions refine their stance, and as technology itself evolves, these challenges will be met with new ideas, solutions, and adaptations.

In the grand scheme of things, we're at the beginning of a new chapter, not the end of the book. And like any good story, it's filled with suspense, intrigue, and a cast of characters striving for something better. The plot twists are many, and the ending is yet to be written. The pen is in our hands, and it's up to us to write the next lines. And just like any journey worth taking, it's not the destination that counts, but how we navigate the challenges along the way.

19.5 Key Takeaways

As we wrap up our discussion on the future of cryptocurrencies and blockchain, let's summarize the main points we've covered.

1. **Regulatory Uncertainty:** Different countries have different attitudes towards cryptocurrencies and blockchain. This

makes it challenging for people and businesses to operate on a global scale. The laws are still evolving, and there's a need for a unified approach.
2. **Technical Limitations:** Scalability is a big issue. Current systems can slow down or become expensive to use when many people jump on board. Solving this problem is crucial for mass adoption.
3. **Security Concerns:** Keeping digital assets safe is an ongoing battle. Hackers are always looking for weaknesses, so constant vigilance and improvement in security measures are necessary.
4. **Economic Volatility:** The value of cryptocurrencies can swing wildly in a short period, making them risky for the average person. Long-term stability is something that still needs to be addressed.
5. **Public Perception:** Many people are still skeptical or unaware of the potential benefits of cryptocurrencies and blockchain. Education and awareness are key to overcoming this hurdle.
6. **Environmental Impact:** The energy usage of some cryptocurrencies has raised concerns about their environmental impact. Solutions are being explored, but finding an eco-friendly alternative is still a work in progress.
7. **Information Gap:** Misinformation or lack of information can hinder the growth and acceptance of cryptocurrencies and blockchain. Accurate, accessible education is crucial.
8. **Ethical and Social Issues:** The technology can be used for both good and bad. Balancing innovation with ethical considerations is a complex challenge.
9. **Future-Proofing:** The tech landscape changes quickly. For these technologies to stand the test of time, they need to be adaptable and ready for future challenges.
10. **The Journey Continues:** The story of cryptocurrencies and blockchain is still unfolding. It's filled with challenges, but also full of opportunities for those willing to engage and innovate.

The road ahead is long and filled with obstacles, but remember, the best journeys are the ones where you learn and grow. As this field evolves, it will continue to face challenges, but it's through overcoming these challenges that progress is made. The story isn't over; in fact, a new chapter is just beginning. And like any compelling story, the most exciting parts are yet to come.

Section 20: Your Next Steps

So, you've made it this far, through the winding and sometimes complex world of cryptocurrencies and blockchain technology. The digital landscape might have seemed like a sprawling jungle at first, but hopefully, the journey has turned it into more of a navigable map. However, understanding the lay of the land is just the beginning. Now comes the real adventure—putting your knowledge into action.

Taking the next steps might feel daunting. It's like standing at the edge of a mysterious forest, filled with both treasures and challenges, not knowing exactly which path to take. But remember, the most rewarding journeys often start with a single, calculated step.

Let's break it down. You've learned about the basics—what cryptocurrencies are, how blockchain works, and even the nitty-gritty stuff like market cap and volume. You've waded through the important but foggy waters of regulation, taxes, and risks. You've glimpsed into smart contracts, decentralized applications, and the futuristic world of Initial Coin Offerings. So what's left?

What's left is the you-part of the equation. The decisions you make from this point forward will shape your experience in this fast-evolving world. You could become an investor, diving into the fluctuating seas of cryptocurrency markets. You could become a developer, crafting smart contracts and decentralized apps that could potentially change the way we interact with the digital realm. Or you might just be an enthusiastic supporter, helping to educate friends and family, and being part of the larger community pushing for innovation and adoption.

So, how do you decide your next steps? Well, you start by evaluating your goals. Are you looking for financial gains, or are you more attracted to the technological side of things? Maybe you're drawn to the idea of decentralization and want to contribute to projects that aim for a more balanced distribution of power and resources. Your goals will guide your path, like a compass in the wilderness.

Now, since the cryptocurrency and blockchain field is still young, it's also a bit like the Wild West—lawless, risky, but filled with opportunities. That means you'll need to be cautious. This isn't a realm where you can afford to wander aimlessly; you'll need to be alert, prepared, and armed with the best tools and information. Each choice you make, whether it's the cryptocurrencies you invest in or the blockchain projects you support, will have its own set of risks and rewards.

At the same time, the landscape is ever-changing. The choices you make today could be reshaped by new regulations tomorrow or technological advancements the day after. Being adaptable is not just an advantage; it's a necessity. You'll need to keep learning, keep questioning, and keep refining your strategies.

What makes this journey especially thrilling is that you're not alone. You're part of a burgeoning community of individuals and organizations, all seeking to shape the future in their own way. Whether online or in-person, these connections can be invaluable. They can provide insights you hadn't considered, strategies you hadn't encountered, and even partnerships that could elevate your journey to new heights.

As we delve into this final section, we'll look at some of the most practical and actionable steps you can take. We'll talk about where you can further your education, how to engage with the community, what resources are at your disposal, and much more. Because understanding is just the start; application is the key.

So, buckle up. The real journey is about to begin. Your next steps could lead you to places you've never imagined, challenge you in ways you never expected, and reward you in manners you never dreamt possible. And while the path won't always be smooth, every twist and turn holds a lesson, every challenge is a test of your mettle, and every victory—no matter how small—adds to your story in this fascinating world.

Welcome to your next chapter. Let's make it a memorable one.

20.1 Learning Resources

You've reached a crucial point in your journey through the realm of cryptocurrencies and blockchain. Knowledge is your most powerful tool here, and just like a craftsman never stops honing their skills, you should never stop learning. Now that you have a good base, where can you go to keep building your knowledge? Thankfully, there are a ton of resources out there, each tailored to different interests, skill levels, and learning styles. Let's dig in.

Books

Sometimes, the old ways are the best ways. Books may be traditional, but they often offer a depth of insight that's hard to find elsewhere. Authors spend months or even years researching, so when you read a book, you're tapping into a concentrated form of wisdom. Whether it's the history of cryptocurrencies, the mechanics of blockchain, or investment strategies, there's probably a book for that. Don't skip the classics like "The Bitcoin Standard" or "Cryptoassets." They offer timeless insights that can help shape your understanding.

Online Courses

The internet is like a sprawling city filled with schools. Online courses are a super accessible way to deepen your knowledge. Websites like

Coursera, Udemy, and edX offer courses on everything from the basics of blockchain to advanced cryptography. The beauty of online courses? You can go at your own pace. So, whether you're a night owl or an early bird, learning can fit into your schedule.

Blogs and Articles

Think of these as your daily news feed for all things crypto and blockchain. Websites like Medium, TechCrunch, and specialized blockchain news outlets offer articles that range from opinion pieces to deep-dive analyses. The best part? Most of these are free. They're perfect for keeping up with the rapid developments in the crypto world. But remember, not all articles are created equal. Always check for credibility and consider multiple viewpoints.

YouTube and Podcasts

Some people learn better by listening or watching rather than reading. If that sounds like you, the world of crypto podcasts and YouTube channels is your playground. From interviews with industry experts to breakdowns of complex topics, these platforms offer a more dynamic way to absorb information. Just plug in your headphones and learn while you're doing chores, exercising, or even commuting.

Webinars and Workshops

Live webinars and workshops add another layer to your learning. They're interactive, allowing you to ask questions and get immediate answers. Many organizations and experts in the field host periodic webinars. Some are free; others might require a fee or a subscription. But the interactive experience often makes it worth it.

Forums and Social Media

Places like Reddit, Twitter, and specialized online forums are the bustling marketplaces of ideas. You can follow thought leaders, join discussions, and even debate on topics that interest you. But a word of caution: the quality of information can vary wildly. Always double-check facts and be wary of following advice blindly.

Conferences and Meetups

Nothing beats the power of face-to-face interaction. Conferences, although sometimes expensive, offer unparalleled access to experts, industry leaders, and like-minded enthusiasts. Then there are local meetups, which might be smaller but are often more personal. These gatherings can be goldmines for networking and can provide you with insights you won't find online.

Research Papers and Journals

If you're the academic type who likes to delve deep into topics, research papers and academic journals could be up your alley. Websites like Google Scholar or databases like JSTOR can provide you with peer-reviewed papers on a multitude of crypto and blockchain topics. It's heavy reading, for sure, but the information is as credible as it gets.

Documentaries

For visual learners who want a comprehensive view without reading through hundreds of pages, documentaries can be an ideal resource. Films like "Banking on Bitcoin" offer historical context, while others focus on specific aspects like the technology or the social impact of cryptocurrencies.

Mentors and Advisors

Last but definitely not least, consider finding a mentor or advisor. This is someone with more experience and knowledge who can guide you, offer advice, and perhaps most importantly, help you avoid common pitfalls. A good mentor can sometimes be the shortcut to understanding complex topics, saving you time and possibly even money.

So, how do you choose which resources to pursue? Think about what you want to achieve. Are you looking to invest? Maybe focus on books and articles about market trends and investment strategies. Interested in the tech side of things? Online courses and workshops on coding for blockchain could be your go-to. And if you're just generally curious, a mix of all these resources can offer a well-rounded education.

But here's the thing: the field of cryptocurrencies and blockchain is still new. It's like a river that keeps changing its course. What's considered groundbreaking today may become outdated tomorrow. Staying updated is not just a one-time effort; it's an ongoing process.

You now have a treasure trove of resources at your fingertips. Use them wisely, be selective, and always keep that mind of yours open and ready to learn. The crypto and blockchain universe is vast, but with the right tools, you can navigate it like a pro.

20.2 How to Buy Your First Crypto

By now, you've learned a lot about the world of cryptocurrencies. You've waded through history, navigated technology, and peeked into the future. You might be asking, "What's the next step?" Well, for many, the next logical step is to actually buy some cryptocurrency. This is where theory meets practice, where you take your first real step into the world of crypto.

Before we dive into the "how-to," let's be clear on one thing: buying cryptocurrency is a financial decision. Like any investment, it carries risks. This isn't like buying a video game or a pair of shoes online. Think of it more like buying a small piece of a company, a fragment of a digital treasure chest, or a slice of a much larger pie. And like all pies, it can be delicious or it could leave a bad taste in your mouth. So proceed carefully, wisely, and never invest more than you can afford to lose.

1. Do Your Homework

Yep, more studying. Sorry to break it to you, but plunging headfirst into crypto without doing your homework could be a recipe for disaster. There are thousands of cryptocurrencies available. Some are strong and promising, while others... not so much. Take time to read up on the ones you're interested in. Are they widely accepted? What problem do they solve? What do experts say about them? Knowledge is your ally here.

2. Choose the Right Exchange

Just like a traditional market where you might buy fruits or clothes, cryptocurrencies are bought and sold on platforms called exchanges. These are like the supermarkets of the digital financial world. Not all exchanges are created equal, though. Some are simple but offer fewer options. Others are complex but offer a wide variety of cryptocurrencies. And remember, just because an exchange is popular doesn't mean it's the right fit for you. Compare fees, security features, and customer reviews before making your choice.

3. Secure Your Investment

Here comes the important part: security. Cryptocurrencies are stored in a digital wallet. Think of it like a high-tech version of a purse or wallet you might carry in your pocket. Your digital wallet can be online, on your computer, or even on a specialized piece of hardware. Research the pros and cons of each to find what best suits your needs. But whatever you do, protect your wallet like it's a treasure chest. Because, in many ways, it is.

4. Register and Get Verified

You've chosen your exchange. Now, it's time to set up an account. This will involve providing some basic information. In many cases, you'll need to verify your identity by uploading documents like a passport or driver's license. Don't rush through this. Make sure all your details are correct. And remember, your account is like a digital version of a bank account, so treat it with the same level of seriousness and security.

5. Make Your First Purchase

You've made it to the big moment. You're ready to make your first purchase. Depending on the exchange, you can buy crypto using regular money (called fiat currency), or you might need to buy one type of cryptocurrency first (like Bitcoin) and then use it to buy others. Some exchanges allow you to buy with a credit card, bank transfer, or even cash. Choose your payment method, decide how much you want to buy, and go through the necessary steps to complete the purchase.

6. Store and Manage Your Crypto

Once you've made the purchase, your new crypto will appear in your digital wallet. You can leave it there, transfer it to another wallet, or use it for various online transactions. Some people buy crypto as a long-term investment, while others actively trade to try to make a profit. Whatever your strategy, keep a close eye on your investment. Markets can be volatile, and the value of your crypto can fluctuate widely.

7. Taxes and Record-Keeping

Yes, taxes. Most countries treat cryptocurrencies as taxable assets. This means you'll need to keep records of your transactions. Depending on where you live, you might have to pay taxes on any gains you make. It's a good idea to consult a tax advisor who understands cryptocurrencies. Don't overlook this part; failing to report could land you in trouble.

8. Stay Updated

As we said before, the crypto world is ever-changing. New developments happen all the time. Make it a habit to stay updated. Follow news, join online communities, and keep learning. Remember, buying your first crypto isn't the end of your journey, it's just the beginning.

And there you have it. You're not just a spectator anymore; you're a participant in the dynamic, often exhilarating world of cryptocurrencies. It's a world that's as full of possibilities as it is of pitfalls. But you're equipped with knowledge, and that's the best tool you can have.

So take that step, but tread wisely. There are treasures to be found in the world of crypto, but like any treasure, they are guarded by challenges, and you're just getting started on this extraordinary quest. Good luck.

20.3 Where to Find Reliable Information

In a world buzzing with noise, rumors, and flashy headlines, finding reliable information is like searching for a needle in a haystack. The landscape of cryptocurrencies is complex and ever-changing. How do you know what's real and what's fake? How do you sift through all the chatter to find the nuggets of truth?

When it comes to cryptocurrencies and the blockchain, this challenge is even greater. Here, technology moves at breakneck speed, laws are always evolving, and a wrong step could cost you. So, where do you go to find trustworthy information? Let's dig into that.

1. Official Websites and Whitepapers

Let's start with the basics. When you hear about a new cryptocurrency or a major update to an existing one, go straight to the source: the official website. These websites usually offer an array of resources to help you understand their project. The most valuable of these is often the whitepaper—a detailed document that outlines everything from the project's goals and technology to its governance and future plans. But remember, even official documents can be misleading or overly optimistic. Always cross-reference what you read.

2. Financial News Websites

Websites like Forbes, The Wall Street Journal, and Bloomberg often cover significant events in the crypto world. Their articles are usually well-researched and provide different perspectives on market trends and innovations. However, keep an eye out for the publication date and consider the credibility of the authors. News gets old fast in the crypto world, and yesterday's information might not be relevant today.

3. Social Media and Online Forums

Sites like Twitter, Reddit, and specialized blockchain forums are breeding grounds for discussion and debate. Here, you can get a sense of public sentiment, learn from other people's experiences, and even ask your own questions. But tread carefully. Anyone can say anything on these platforms, and it's easy to get caught in the hype or become a victim of misinformation. Use these resources to gather diverse opinions but confirm any claims through more reliable channels.

4. Industry Blogs and Influencers

Many industry experts run blogs or YouTube channels where they share their insights and analyses. While these can be rich sources of information, remember that even experts have biases and opinions. Some may even be paid to promote particular cryptocurrencies. Always cross-reference their information and consider the biases they may have.

5. Online Courses and Webinars

If you're new to this realm or looking to deepen your understanding, consider taking an online course. Websites like Coursera, Udemy, and even some universities offer courses on cryptocurrencies and blockchain. Webinars can also be valuable, especially those hosted by renowned experts in the field.

6. Government and Regulatory Websites

Don't forget about the rule-makers and gatekeepers. Government websites and financial regulatory bodies often release guidelines, laws, and opinions concerning cryptocurrencies. This information is especially crucial if you're looking to understand the legal implications of your crypto activities.

7. Academic Papers and Journals

For those who really want to get into the nitty-gritty, academic papers can provide deep insights into specific topics. Researchers often delve into complex issues like security vulnerabilities, economic models, and technical innovations in the blockchain. However, academic papers are often difficult to read and may require a certain level of expertise to fully understand.

8. Peer Reviews and Community Feedback

Never underestimate the power of community wisdom. Websites that allow users to review and rank different cryptocurrencies, wallets, and exchanges can provide a wealth of knowledge. These reviews often cover essential points like ease of use, security, and customer service. But just like restaurant reviews, take them with a grain of salt. A single bad experience doesn't define an entire platform.

9. Books and Long-Form Guides

Sometimes, you need more than an article or a video to understand the complexities of the crypto world. Numerous books offer comprehensive guides to blockchain technology, investing in cryptocurrencies, and the future of digital assets. Take your time with these; they can be invaluable resources.

10. Trusted Friends and Advisors

Lastly, if you're lucky enough to have friends or family members who are knowledgeable about crypto, don't hesitate to seek their advice. Personal experiences can offer insights that you won't find in any article or forum. However, keep in mind that what worked for someone else might not work for you.

In the end, the key to finding reliable information is to look in multiple places, think critically, and always keep learning. The world of cryptocurrencies is vast and varied. Some days, you'll feel like a detective, piecing together clues to make sense of it all. Other days, you'll feel like a pioneer, stepping into new territories that few have explored.

Whatever the case, remember that in this digital treasure hunt, knowledge is your most valuable asset. Equip yourself with it, and you'll be better prepared to navigate the fascinating, complicated, and ever-changing world of cryptocurrencies.

20.4 How to Keep Learning

So, you've dipped your toes into the swirling waters of cryptocurrencies. Maybe you've even dived in a little deeper. The question is, how do you keep going? How do you keep learning in a landscape that seems to change as quickly as the weather?

1. Stay Curious

The first thing to remember is that learning never stops. Even experts in the field will tell you they're always learning. It's like being a detective; there's always another clue to follow, another case to solve. But for that, you need a detective's best friend: curiosity. Ask questions, seek answers, and don't settle for what you think you know.

2. Follow News Outlets

Staying up-to-date with the latest developments is crucial. New technologies emerge, laws change, and markets fluctuate. Websites and newsletters that focus on cryptocurrencies can keep you informed. Just like a morning newspaper, make it a routine to catch up on the crypto world each day or each week. And don't just stick to one source; multiple viewpoints can offer a fuller picture.

3. Join Online Communities

The Internet is full of places where people talk about cryptocurrencies. These could be specialized forums, subreddits, or even Facebook groups. However, remember that not all voices in these communities are equal. Just like in a noisy market square, some people know what they're talking about, and others are just making noise. Learn to separate the wisdom from the chatter.

4. Engage in Projects and Challenges

One of the best ways to learn is by doing. Numerous online platforms offer coding challenges, trading simulations, and other activities related to cryptocurrencies and blockchain. Imagine you're an apprentice, and each task is a lesson from a master craftsman. These hands-on experiences can provide invaluable insights into how things work.

5. Read Books and Articles

Long-form content, like books and in-depth articles, can provide insights that news reports or social media updates just can't. Think of it as diving deeper into the ocean instead of just skimming the surface. Many books cover a wide range of topics from the basics of blockchain to the ethics of cryptocurrencies. Consider setting a reading goal, like one new book every month or a set number of articles per week.

6. Take Online Courses

Remember those days in school when a subject only became clear because of a great teacher? Some things never change. Online courses can be like having a personal tutor in cryptocurrencies. Websites like Coursera, Udemy, and even YouTube offer a range of courses on various topics related to the crypto world. Some are free, while others require payment or a subscription. The key is to find courses that suit your learning style and needs.

7. Attend Conferences and Webinars

If you can, attending conferences, even virtual ones, can be like stepping into a different world—a world full of experts, innovations, and new ideas. These events often feature talks from leading figures in the field, panel discussions, and even hands-on workshops. It's also an opportunity to network with like-minded individuals. Even if you can't attend in person, many conferences offer live streams or recordings of their events.

8. Network with Experts

Building relationships with people who are already experts can provide a treasure trove of knowledge and experience. Social media platforms like LinkedIn can be a good starting point for connecting with professionals in the field. Sometimes, a single conversation with an expert can offer insights that you won't find in any book or article.

9. Watch and Listen

Aside from reading and doing, there's also watching and listening. Many podcasts and video channels are dedicated to cryptocurrencies. Whether you're cooking, commuting, or just relaxing, you can tune in to hear experts discuss the latest trends, share insights, and even debate contentious topics. Make it a point to follow a couple of reputable podcasts or YouTube channels.

10. Review and Reflect

Let's not forget the importance of looking back. Occasionally take the time to review what you've learned. Go back to your old questions and see if you can answer them now. Revisit previous assumptions and see if they still hold up. It's like checking a map to see how far you've come and which direction to take next.

11. Experiment Safely

If you're ready, you might want to try investing a small amount in cryptocurrencies or building a simple blockchain application. It's like learning to swim; sometimes you have to get wet. But remember to do so safely. Start small, be cautious, and always follow the best security practices.

12. Keep an Open Mind

Last but certainly not least, keep an open mind. The world of cryptocurrencies is filled with differing opinions, controversial issues, and endless possibilities. An open mind will help you navigate through disagreements and challenges, and allow you to see opportunities where others see obstacles.

Remember, in this vast, intricate, and often puzzling universe of cryptocurrencies, you're both a student and an explorer. The road may be long, and the journey may be challenging, but each step takes you closer to understanding this transformative technology. And in a field that's writing its history as we speak, who knows—you might even end up being one of its authors.

20.5 Key Takeaways

Alright, we've traveled a long road together in the world of cryptocurrencies. Let's take a moment to reflect on what we've learned in this final section, "Your Next Steps," before you set out on your own adventures.

1. **Never Stop Learning:** The crypto universe is always changing. To keep up, you need to make learning a constant part of your routine.

2. **Diverse Information Sources:** From news outlets and books to online courses and webinars, using a range of sources will give you a well-rounded understanding.
3. **Hands-On Experience:** There's no substitute for practical experience. Engage in projects, take on challenges, and experiment (safely) to gain invaluable insights.
4. **Community Engagement:** Join online forums and social media groups that focus on crypto topics. Be discerning in choosing reliable sources and separating wisdom from noise.
5. **Networking:** Build relationships with people who are already in the field. Networking can open doors and provide insights that are not available through other learning resources.
6. **Conferences and Events:** These gatherings, whether in-person or virtual, can offer deep dives into specialized topics and opportunities to learn from experts.
7. **Review and Reflect:** Periodically look back at what you've learned, reassess your understanding, and adjust your learning path accordingly.
8. **Be Curious and Open-Minded:** Ask questions, challenge your own assumptions, and be open to new ideas and technologies.
9. **Safety and Caution:** When experimenting, especially with investments or coding projects, always proceed with caution and adhere to best practices in security.
10. **Continuous Growth:** Set achievable goals and take actionable steps toward them. This includes reading goals, course completion, or even investment milestones.

In a realm as dynamic and evolving as cryptocurrencies, each of these points can serve as a compass to guide you. You might not know where exactly you're headed—and that's okay. Uncertainty is part of the adventure. What matters is that you're equipped with the right tools and the right mindset to navigate whatever comes your way.

You're no longer just a spectator; you're a participant in this grand, complex tale of technology, economics, and human behavior. And remember, every participant has the potential to become a leader or even a game-changer. So, are you ready for your next steps?

Conclusion

So here we are, standing at the edge of a frontier that is as thrilling as it is bewildering. From the beginnings of Bitcoin to the future potentials and pitfalls of blockchain technology, we've journeyed through the intricate maze of cryptocurrencies together.

Maybe you're feeling a bit like a miner from the Gold Rush days—excited but cautious, armed with tools but not entirely sure what to expect. The truth is, no one can predict the future of cryptocurrencies with certainty. It's like a weather system—complex and influenced by many factors we can't fully grasp. Yet, understanding the system itself can help you navigate through it more confidently.

Let's remember some of the ground we've covered:

1. **The Basics:** We dived deep into the nuts and bolts of what makes cryptocurrencies tick. We saw how they're different from traditional currencies, how they work, and what fuels them.
2. **Blockchain:** This technology is the backbone of cryptocurrencies. It's more than a trend; it's a paradigm shift that could revolutionize various industries.
3. **Trading and Investments:** You got a crash course on trading, market trends, risks, and even some strategies to protect yourself from market volatility.
4. **Technology and Tools:** We looked at wallets, exchanges, and even got into the nitty-gritty of some technologies like smart contracts and decentralized applications (DApps).
5. **Risks and Regulations:** It's not all sunshine and rainbows. We discussed the risks involved, both from a market and a regulatory standpoint, so you're not caught off guard.
6. **The Future:** Lastly, we had a glimpse of the ever-changing landscape and the potential for massive shifts in the world as

we know it, thanks to cryptocurrencies and blockchain technology.

Each of these pieces is like a thread woven into the fabric of this larger narrative about the impact of technology on society, economy, and our daily lives. Whether you're an investor, a techie, or someone just trying to understand what all the fuss is about, these threads come together to create a tapestry that is hard to ignore.

But here's the kicker: this tapestry is still being woven. The loom of time and progress doesn't stop. New patterns emerge, old threads fray and break, and the whole tapestry takes on new shapes. What does that mean for you? It means that your understanding, your involvement, your risks and gains—none of them are static. They will change as you learn and grow, and as the world of cryptocurrencies itself expands and matures.

What also changes is your responsibility. The more you know, the more you're equipped to make sound decisions. But that also means you're more responsible for those decisions. Ignorance may be bliss, but knowledge, when applied wisely, is power. And with power comes responsibility. So as you step further into this realm, remember that you're not just a passive observer; you're an active participant. Your actions, however small, contribute to this ever-evolving space.

And there's something quite remarkable about that, isn't there? That each of us, armed with a little bit of knowledge and a whole lot of curiosity, can be a part of something much larger than ourselves. It's like adding a pebble to a growing mountain. Your pebble may seem insignificant, but collectively, it all adds up to something monumental.

But what if you're still uncertain? What if you still have a thousand questions swirling in your head? That's okay. Uncertainty is a sign that there's more to learn, that there are more avenues to explore. It's not a roadblock; it's a stepping stone.

Remember, cryptocurrencies and blockchain technology didn't just appear overnight. They are the product of years of innovation, trial and error, and yes, even some failures. So, as you make your way through this exciting but complex world, it's alright to have doubts. It's alright to make mistakes. What's important is that you keep moving, keep questioning, and keep learning.

In a realm that's as multifaceted as this, your best asset is an open mind. You may not have all the answers, and that's fine. Neither does anyone else. But by embracing the uncertainty and being willing to learn, you're already several steps ahead of those who choose to remain in the dark.

So, as we wrap up this extensive journey, remember that this is not the end. It's just the beginning of your unique path in the dynamic world of cryptocurrencies. What comes next is entirely up to you.

Final Thoughts

Here we are, at the end of a journey that has taken us through the winding roads and intricate details of the world of cryptocurrencies and blockchain technology. It's been a learning expedition, filled with wonder, caution, and most importantly, a treasure trove of knowledge. It's like finishing a book that you just can't put down, only to find out that the story continues—just in a different format. Your format.

We've explored the past, present, and even peered into the future. We've discussed the technical aspects, the financial implications, and the regulatory frameworks. We've touched on risks, opportunities, and the huge potential for both societal gain and individual growth. It's a lot to digest, but it's vital if you're going to navigate these choppy waters successfully.

Cryptocurrencies are not just a trend. They're part of a larger conversation about what our future could look like. They're the voice in a choir that's singing a song of change, innovation, and endless possibilities. But like any form of change, they come with their own set of challenges. And how you face these challenges—equipped with the knowledge and wisdom you've gained—will define your journey ahead.

In many ways, the act of learning about this realm is like holding a double-edged sword. On one edge is the thrill of discovery, and on the other is the weight of responsibility. It's not just about knowing; it's about applying what you know in a way that is ethical, sensible, and mindful of the bigger picture. You're not just a spectator in this evolving story; you're a character with a role to play. And your actions, your decisions, and your voice matter.

There's a saying that knowledge is power, but I'd like to add to that: "Knowledge is power, but wisdom is empowerment." It's not enough to simply accumulate facts and figures. It's about understanding the implications, the whys and hows, and making informed choices that benefit not just you, but the larger community as well.

As you step forward into your next chapter in the world of cryptocurrencies, carry this knowledge like a torch—it'll light your way but also cast shadows. Be aware of those shadows, those areas still hidden from your understanding, and strive to illuminate them. There will always be more to learn, more to discover, and more to understand. That's not a flaw; it's a feature. It's what makes this journey so incredibly engaging.

So, as you close this book—both literally and metaphorically—remember that your education doesn't stop here. It evolves, just like the world of cryptocurrencies and blockchain technology will continue to evolve. And just like these digital currencies are decentralized, remember that the power to influence, to contribute, and to make a difference is decentralized too. It lies with each of us.

Your next steps aren't written yet, but the pen is in your hand. What will your story be?

And with that, dear reader, we bid adieu to this chapter, but not to the journey. The road ahead is long, but as you've seen, it's one worth traveling. Safe travels, and may your path be illuminated by the light of wisdom and curiosity.

Next Steps

So, you've reached the end of this comprehensive guide, but as we've mentioned before, the journey doesn't stop here. Think of this as your base camp, a place where you've gathered essential knowledge and resources. Now it's time to take what you've learned and put it into action. Below are some concrete steps to help you continue on your path.

Expand Your Knowledge

You've learned the basics and even delved into some more complex topics. But the world of cryptocurrencies and blockchain is constantly changing. New technologies and regulations emerge, and it's crucial to stay updated. Subscribe to reputable blogs, podcasts, and journals that focus on these topics.

Practice Safe Investing

If you're considering investing in cryptocurrencies, remember the advice on being a responsible investor. Diversify your portfolio, understand your risk tolerance, and never invest money you can't afford to lose. Consulting with a financial advisor who understands cryptocurrencies can be a wise decision.

Engage with the Community

Cryptocurrencies and blockchain technology have strong communities, both online and offline. Engaging with these communities can provide you with new perspectives, practical advice, and even potential partnerships for projects. You're not alone on this journey, and there's much to be gained by walking this path with others.

Develop Skills

Whether you're looking to become a developer, a trader, or just a well-informed citizen, there are skills to be acquired. Consider taking online courses or attending workshops. Your career path in this field could start with becoming more specialized in a particular area of interest.

Advocate and Educate

The more people understand about cryptocurrencies and blockchain, the less stigma and misunderstanding there will be. If you've found this information valuable, share it with friends, family, and colleagues. You might just help someone else take their first steps into this exciting world.

Regulatory Watch

Keep an eye on the ever-changing landscape of laws and regulations concerning cryptocurrencies. Even a small change can have a big impact on the market and your investments. Being informed is being prepared.

Experiment and Innovate

You've learned about Smart Contracts, DApps, and ICOs. If you have an idea, why not prototype it? There are many open-source resources available to help you bring your visions to life.

Keep Security Front and Center

Never underestimate the importance of cybersecurity. Secure your investments, protect your information, and be vigilant against scams and frauds. This is a shared responsibility for everyone in the community.

In conclusion, your next steps are your own, but they don't have to be taken alone or without preparation. The road ahead is as exciting as it is challenging. As you venture forward into the complex world of cryptocurrencies and blockchain, take your time, tread carefully, but never cease to marvel at the possibilities that await.

This is your story now. You're equipped to write the next chapters. How they unfold is up to you. Thank you for letting us be a part of your journey so far. We wish you nothing but success and enlightenment as you move forward.

And so, dear reader, this may be where our guide ends, but your adventure is just beginning. Take that step, there's a whole world waiting for you.

■

THE END

Glossary

Address: A string of characters used to send and receive cryptocurrency. Similar to a bank account number in traditional finance, it identifies where a transaction originates or where it is being sent.

Altcoin: Any cryptocurrency other than Bitcoin. Examples include Ethereum, Ripple (XRP), and Litecoin.

AML (Anti-Money Laundering): Laws and regulations designed to prevent illegal activities like money laundering by tracking and monitoring financial transactions, including those involving cryptocurrencies.

Blockchain: A decentralized, distributed ledger that records transactions across many computers in such a way that the registered transactions cannot be altered retroactively. It is the underlying technology behind cryptocurrencies.

Cold Wallet: A type of cryptocurrency wallet that is stored offline, such as on a hardware device or paper. Cold wallets are considered more secure than hot wallets because they are less vulnerable to hacking.

Consensus Mechanism: The process by which participants in a blockchain network agree on the validity of transactions. Examples include Proof of Work (PoW) and Proof of Stake (PoS).

Cryptocurrency: A digital or virtual currency that uses cryptography for security. It operates independently of a central authority, such as a bank or government.

DApp (Decentralized Application): An application that runs on a decentralized network, typically a blockchain. Unlike traditional apps, DApps are not controlled by a single entity.

Decentralization: The distribution of power and control away from a central authority. In the context of blockchain and cryptocurrencies, it means that no single entity controls the network.

ERC-20: A standard protocol for tokens on the Ethereum blockchain. Most of the tokens created on Ethereum follow this standard, making them easily interchangeable and compatible with each other.

Exchange: A platform where cryptocurrencies can be bought, sold, or traded. Exchanges can be centralized (controlled by a single entity) or decentralized (peer-to-peer).

Fiat Currency: Government-issued currency that is not backed by a physical commodity, such as gold or silver, but rather by the government that issues it. Examples include the US Dollar, Euro, and Japanese Yen.

Fork: A split in the blockchain network that results in two separate versions of the blockchain. This can occur as a result of a protocol change, disagreement among developers, or to create a new cryptocurrency.

Gas: A unit that measures the amount of computational effort required to perform operations on the Ethereum blockchain. Users must pay gas fees to execute transactions or run smart contracts.

Halving: An event in which the reward for mining new blocks is reduced by half. This occurs approximately every four years in Bitcoin and is designed to control the supply of new coins.

Hardware Wallet: A physical device used to store cryptocurrencies offline. It provides an extra layer of security by keeping private keys separate from online, potentially vulnerable environments.

Hash: A fixed-length string of characters generated from data of any size using a mathematical algorithm. In blockchain, hashing is used to create a unique identifier for each block in the chain.

HODL: A slang term in the cryptocurrency community that means "Hold On for Dear Life." It refers to the strategy of holding onto cryptocurrency investments for a long period, regardless of market volatility.

ICO (Initial Coin Offering): A fundraising method where new cryptocurrencies or tokens are sold to early backers in exchange for other cryptocurrencies like Bitcoin or Ethereum. Similar to an IPO (Initial Public Offering) in traditional finance.

Immutable: The characteristic of a blockchain that prevents data from being changed or deleted once it is recorded. This ensures the integrity and transparency of the blockchain.

KYC (Know Your Customer): A regulatory requirement for financial institutions and exchanges to verify the identity of their customers. This is done to prevent illegal activities such as money laundering and fraud.

Liquidity: The ease with which an asset can be bought or sold in the market without affecting its price. In the context of cryptocurrencies, high liquidity means that the asset can be quickly converted to cash or other assets.

Mining: The process of validating and recording transactions on a blockchain network. Miners use computational power to solve complex mathematical problems, and in return, they are rewarded with newly created cryptocurrency.

Node: A computer that is connected to a blockchain network and participates in the process of validating and relaying transactions. Nodes store copies of the blockchain and help maintain its integrity.

NFT (Non-Fungible Token): A unique digital asset that represents ownership of a specific item, such as art, music, or virtual real estate. Unlike cryptocurrencies, NFTs are not interchangeable and each one has its own value.

Peer-to-Peer (P2P): A type of network where participants interact directly with each other without the need for a central authority or intermediary. In cryptocurrencies, P2P transactions are conducted directly between users.

Private Key: A secret code that allows the owner to access and manage their cryptocurrency. It is crucial to keep private keys secure, as anyone with access to the key can control the associated funds.

Proof of Stake (PoS): A consensus mechanism used by some blockchains where validators are chosen to create new blocks based on the number of coins they hold and are willing to "stake" as collateral.

Proof of Work (PoW): A consensus mechanism used by blockchains like Bitcoin, where miners compete to solve complex mathematical problems. The first miner to solve the problem gets to add a new block to the blockchain and is rewarded with cryptocurrency.

Public Key: A cryptographic code that allows users to receive cryptocurrency. It is derived from the private key and can be shared publicly, as it cannot be used to access funds on its own.

Satoshi Nakamoto: The pseudonymous person or group of people who created Bitcoin and wrote its original whitepaper in 2008. The true identity of Satoshi Nakamoto remains unknown.

Scalability: The ability of a blockchain network to handle an increasing number of transactions. Scalability is a major challenge for many cryptocurrencies, especially as they grow in popularity.

Security Token: A type of token that represents ownership of an asset, such as shares in a company or real estate. Security tokens are subject to federal securities regulations, unlike utility tokens, which are not.

Smart Contract: A self-executing contract with the terms of the agreement directly written into code. Smart contracts automatically enforce and execute the terms when certain conditions are met, without the need for intermediaries.

Stablecoin: A type of cryptocurrency that is pegged to the value of a traditional currency, commodity, or a basket of assets. Stablecoins are designed to minimize price volatility, making them more suitable for everyday transactions.

Token: A digital asset issued on a blockchain that can represent ownership, rights, or other forms of value. Tokens can be used for a variety of purposes, such as accessing services, voting in governance, or representing assets.

Volatility: The degree of variation in the price of a cryptocurrency over time. High volatility means that the price can change rapidly and unpredictably, which can lead to significant gains or losses for investors.

Wallet: A digital tool that allows users to store, send, and receive cryptocurrencies. Wallets can be software-based (online or on a computer) or hardware-based (a physical device).

Whitepaper: A detailed document released by a cryptocurrency project that outlines its goals, technology, and plans. The whitepaper is often the first point of reference for potential investors and users.

Whale: A term used to describe an individual or entity that holds a large amount of cryptocurrency. Whales have the potential to influence market prices due to the size of their holdings.

Yield Farming: A process in decentralized finance (DeFi) where users lend or stake their cryptocurrency in exchange for rewards or interest. Yield farming can be highly profitable but also comes with significant risks.

Appendices

The appendices section is designed to provide additional resources, tools, and references to help you dive deeper into the world of cryptocurrencies and blockchain technology. This section includes practical guides, further reading, useful tools, and more, ensuring you have everything you need to continue your journey.

Appendix A: Step-by-Step Guide to Setting Up a Crypto Wallet

1. **Choosing the Right Wallet**:
    - **Types of Wallets**: Hot wallets, cold wallets, hardware wallets, paper wallets.
    - **Recommended Wallets**: A list of popular and reliable wallets, including Ledger, Trezor, MetaMask, and Trust Wallet.
    - **Security Considerations**: Importance of securing your wallet with strong passwords, two-factor authentication, and safe storage of recovery phrases.
2. **Setting Up a Wallet**:
    - **Software Wallet Setup**: Step-by-step instructions for setting up a software wallet, including downloading the app, creating an account, and backing up your recovery phrase.
    - **Hardware Wallet Setup**: Instructions for setting up a hardware wallet, including initialization, creating a PIN, and securely storing the recovery seed.
3. **Sending and Receiving Cryptocurrencies**:
    - **How to Send Crypto**: Detailed steps on sending cryptocurrency from your wallet, including entering the recipient's address, selecting the amount, and confirming the transaction.

- **How to Receive Crypto**: Instructions for generating a receiving address, sharing it with the sender, and confirming the receipt of funds.

Appendix B: Comprehensive List of Exchanges

1. **Centralized Exchanges**:
   - **Binance**: Overview, features, fees, and security measures.
   - **Coinbase**: User-friendliness, supported currencies, and account security.
   - **Kraken**: Advanced trading features, margin trading, and regulatory compliance.
2. **Decentralized Exchanges (DEXs)**:
   - **Uniswap**: How it works, benefits of using a DEX, and liquidity pools.
   - **SushiSwap**: Overview of features, staking, and governance.
   - **PancakeSwap**: Differences from other DEXs, Binance Smart Chain integration, and yield farming options.
3. **Choosing the Right Exchange**:
   - **Factors to Consider**: Liquidity, security, fees, supported cryptocurrencies, and regulatory compliance.
   - **How to Register and Verify**: General steps for signing up, completing KYC (Know Your Customer) verification, and securing your account.

Appendix C: Taxation Guidelines for Cryptocurrencies

1. **Understanding Tax Obligations**:

- **Capital Gains Tax**: How buying, selling, and trading cryptocurrencies are taxed as capital gains.
 - **Income Tax**: When cryptocurrencies received as payment or through mining are considered income and taxed accordingly.
2. **Country-Specific Regulations**:
 - **United States**: IRS guidelines, forms required, and reporting capital gains.
 - **European Union**: Overview of different regulations across EU member states.
 - **Asia**: A look at how countries like Japan, South Korea, and India are taxing cryptocurrencies.
3. **Tax Reporting Tools**:
 - **Crypto Tax Software**: Recommendations for tools like CoinTracker, Koinly, and TokenTax that help automate the process of calculating and reporting taxes on cryptocurrencies.
 - **Record-Keeping Best Practices**: Tips on keeping accurate records of transactions, using CSV files from exchanges, and organizing receipts.

Appendix D: List of Recommended Books and Resources

1. **Books on Cryptocurrencies**:
 - *The Bitcoin Standard* by Saifedean Ammous: A comprehensive look at the history of money and how Bitcoin fits into the financial landscape.
 - *Cryptoassets* by Chris Burniske and Jack Tatar: A guide to investing in cryptocurrencies and understanding their potential as a new asset class.
 - *Mastering Bitcoin* by Andreas M. Antonopoulos: A technical guide for developers, but also valuable for

anyone wanting a deeper understanding of how Bitcoin works.
2. **Online Resources**:
   - **Websites**: CoinMarketCap, CoinGecko, and CoinDesk for market data, news, and analysis.
   - **Forums and Communities**: Reddit's r/CryptoCurrency and BitcoinTalk for discussions and community support.
   - **YouTube Channels**: Andreas Antonopoulos, DataDash, and Coin Bureau for educational videos and market analysis.
3. **Courses and Certifications**:
   - **Coursera**: Introduction to Blockchain and Cryptocurrency by Duke University.
   - **Udemy**: Cryptocurrency Investment Course 2024: Fund Your Retirement!
   - **Blockchain Council**: Certified Blockchain Expert and Certified Cryptocurrency Trader courses.

Appendix E: Frequently Asked Questions (FAQs)

1. **General FAQs**:
   - **What is a Blockchain?**: A brief explanation of blockchain technology and how it works.
   - **How do I buy cryptocurrency?**: Step-by-step guide summarized from earlier sections.
   - **Is cryptocurrency legal?**: Overview of the legal status of cryptocurrencies in major regions around the world.
2. **Security FAQs**:
   - **How do I keep my cryptocurrency safe?**: Tips on using hardware wallets, securing private keys, and avoiding phishing scams.

- **What should I do if I lose my private key?**: Explanation of the consequences and the importance of secure backups.
3. **Investment FAQs**:
    - **What are the risks of investing in cryptocurrency?**: Discussion of volatility, security risks, and regulatory uncertainties.
    - **How can I diversify my crypto portfolio?**: Tips on spreading investments across different cryptocurrencies and other asset classes.

Appendix F: Common Crypto Scams and How to Avoid Them

1. **Types of Scams**:
    - **Phishing Scams**: How scammers trick users into giving up their private keys or login credentials.
    - **Ponzi Schemes**: Recognizing fraudulent investment schemes that promise high returns with little risk.
    - **Fake ICOs**: How to spot and avoid fraudulent Initial Coin Offerings that aim to steal investor funds.
2. **Protective Measures**:
    - **Due Diligence**: Importance of researching projects, teams, and whitepapers before investing.
    - **Security Practices**: Best practices for securing your devices, wallets, and online accounts.
    - **Red Flags**: Warning signs of potential scams, such as unrealistic promises, lack of transparency, and pressure to invest quickly.

Appendix G: Key Historical Events in Cryptocurrency

1. **The Birth of Bitcoin**:
   - **2008**: Publication of the Bitcoin whitepaper by Satoshi Nakamoto.
   - **2009**: The mining of the first Bitcoin block (Genesis Block) and the launch of the Bitcoin network.
2. **Major Milestones**:
   - **2010**: The first real-world Bitcoin transaction (Bitcoin Pizza Day).
   - **2013**: The rise and fall of Mt. Gox, one of the earliest Bitcoin exchanges.
   - **2017**: The explosion of ICOs and the cryptocurrency market boom.
3. **Regulatory and Market Shifts**:
   - **2018**: The crypto market crash and subsequent regulatory crackdowns.
   - **2020**: The rise of Decentralized Finance (DeFi) and the mainstream acceptance of cryptocurrencies.

Final Words

Thank you for choosing *Crypto Simplified* as your guide through the fascinating world of cryptocurrencies and blockchain technology. We hope this book has provided you with valuable insights and practical knowledge to confidently navigate this ever-evolving landscape. Your decision to invest in your education and understanding is commendable, and we're honored to have been part of your journey. Keep exploring, stay curious, and remember that this is just the beginning of an exciting adventure. Congratulations on taking this significant step forward, and we wish you all the best in your future endeavors!

www.ingramcontent.com/pod-product-compliance
Lightning Source LLC
Chambersburg PA
CBHW071912210526
45479CB00002B/382